FEARLESS
NEGOTIATING

FEARLESS NEGOTIATING

THE WISH-WANT-WALK METHOD
TO REACH SOLUTIONS
THAT WORK

▲▲▲

MICHAEL C. DONALDSON

McGraw-Hill

New York   Chicago   San Francisco   Lisbon   London
Madrid   Mexico City   Milan   New Delhi   San Juan
Seoul   Singapore   Sydney   Toronto

2 3 4 5 6 7 8 9 0   FGR/FGR   0 9 8 7

ISBN-13: 978-0-07-148779-5
ISBN-10: 0-07-148779-4

> —*From a Declaration of Principles Jointly Adopted*
> *by a Committee of the American Bar Association*
> *and a Committee of Publishers and Associations*

McGraw-Hill books are available at special discounts to use as premiums and sales promotions, or for use in corporate training programs. For more information, please write to the Director of Special Sales, Professional Publishing, McGraw-Hill, Two Penn Plaza, New York, NY 10121-2298. Or contact your local bookstore.

This book is printed on acid-free paper.

This book is dedicated to
Tim Kittleson
for keeping me on track and on target.

CONTENTS

FOREWORD

▲ ▲ ▲

As the leader of a $1 billion corporation, I face the typical challenges confronting the CEO of any professional services organization of similar size. Perhaps somewhat unique to my particular leadership angst, however, is the fact that my company comprises some 6,000 highly educated professionals located in more than 170 independent offices in 34 countries around the globe, who must deal with several distinctive client sets within different levels of government and in commercial industry.

While all of our global team members are passionate about technology, not as many have had formal business training, especially at the client relationship level. Hence, most have an aversion to the idea of client contract negotiation, tending more toward the view of profit as an "evil necessity." As CEO, I view profit as the lifeblood of corporate survival, not to mention vital to the ability to reward the expertise and talent of our team members.

Being somewhat of a corporate maverick, I have always been interested in cultural change. Nelson

Mandela is quoted as saying, "Education is the most powerful weapon which you can use to change the world." With only the aspiration of changing our corporate culture in mind, we established an internal corporate university to educate team members on business best practices spanning all client and service lines.

It was easy to recognize that 80 percent of our end profit came from negotiating original contract conditions: Good contracts produce greater profit than good managers alone can do. Therefore, contract negotiation became a crucial subject for our corporate university. Fortunately, we tapped Michael Donaldson to facilitate our course on pricing and negotiation.

Our objectives were that the course be:

- effective, yet simple enough to be mastered in a short, three-day period;

- broad enough to benefit our company across different client sets and services; and

- compelling enough to be embraced by technological professionals who are honored to apply their expertise to satisfy clients' needs, but who dread the requisite contract negotiations.

Michael's methodology has been easy to understand and replicate. It has provided our team members with a powerful, clear-cut, common sense approach that is easy to remember and apply—one that works to minimize client conflict and arrive at better contracts. Perhaps best of all, it has yielded millions of dollars in increased profits, resulting in healthier budgets and freeing our technological professionals to focus on satisfying and retaining clients.

For any endeavor, business or otherwise, that depends on quality contracts, the potential return on investment of Michael Donaldson's "Wish-Want-Walk" negotiation method is virtually infinite.

Bob Uhler
President and CEO
MWH Global, Inc.—
*Dedicated to creating a sustainable business
for Building a Better World*

FEARLESS
NEGOTIATING

INTRODUCTION

WELCOME TO THE WISH-WANT-WALK method of negotiating. This book is designed to take the angst out of any negotiation in which you will take part. Turning every reader of this book into a fearless negotiator sounds like a tall order, but this method has been used for everything from relatively simple negotiations like buying a car or a house to getting a raise, as well as negotiating complex, international, multi-party contracts for projects that will take years to build. The Wish-Want-Walk method works from the bedroom to the boardroom and all around the world.

The Wish-Want-Walk method has been used in such a wide variety of negotiations that we know it works, every time. I will provide many examples from real life in these pages. Wish, Want, Walk also acts as a highly accurate predictor of the outcome of a negotiation. In fact, during the mock negotiations that are conducted in my seminars, I like to predict the result of the negotiation for the various teams and even pick out the teams that will not close a deal. I have a surprisingly good batting average. Exactly how that works will also be explained.

This method also gives you a handy tool to evaluate a negotiation objectively after it is over. Many people rank a negotiation by how they feel emotionally when it is finished. If you were yelled at, the negotiation is a bitter memory no matter what the results. If you felt good about the other person after the negotiation, you also probably felt good about the result of the negotiation no matter how much you left on the table. Other people will rank their negotiation by comparing the result they achieved to the result someone else achieved for a similar product or service. They beat themselves up if a friend bought a similar item for less. The Wish-Want-Walk method will give you the tools to make a more objective and consistent evaluation of every negotiation.

The best part of this approach is that you will be much more comfortable when you take Wish, Want, Walk with you into the negotiating room. It will literally be your guide in the room. It is like having someone whispering in your ear. It tells you where to start the bidding and when to call it quits. For that reason it produces the results you want more often than any other single tool you can possibly possess. You will see for yourself. That is the experience—reported from many folks from all sorts of businesses—that gave birth to the title of this book, *Fearless Negotiating*.

This book grew out of the many negotiation seminars that I lead for organizations across the United States, Europe, and Asia. Some of the negotiating seminars last $2\,^1/_2$ hours. Some are three-day intensive workshops that begin at 8:00 a.m. and end at 10:00 p.m. (except the third day ends at 4:30 p.m., sharp). After all that work, the participants consistently say that the single most important thing they take away from the course is making a Wish-Want-Walk plan and sticking to it.

I began teaching negotiation courses in the early 1990s at UCLA in the extension program and later as part of the summer producing program in the School of Theater, Film, and Television. This was a natural way to give back to the community that had been so good to me and to share what I had learned in my professional life. I have been an entertainment lawyer for nearly forty years, representing artists in their dealings with the six major studios that run the film business. Most of them are producers, writers, directors, and people you would not know. Some, like Michael Landon of *Little House on the Prairie* fame and the magician David Copperfield, are names that are known around the world. No matter how well known or successful they might be, my clients usually believe that the studios have all the power. Typically my first job is to convince my clients that it is never true that one side has all the power. Identifying sources of power and how to tap into them are included in this book.

So, who is this book for? It is for:

- anyone who is feeling a bit unsure going into a negotiation

- anyone who feels beaten up after a negotiating session

- anyone who feels that they could have or should have done better in their last negotiation

- anyone who wants to say "Yes" to the master negotiator within each and every one of us

You might be thinking that the book is for just about everybody, and you would be right. But there is one person it is not for. This book is not for my grandson. His name is Soul. He is eight years old. Soul doesn't need this book because he knows how to get just about anything he wants. He is a well-mannered, world-class negotiator, as you were at that age.

The trouble is that as you reach and pass that time in your life, your parents and teachers and other adults have begun to squelch your inner, natural-born negotiator. They tell you that you can't do this and you shouldn't do that. They want you to stop doing a hundred things that tend to annoy them. These messages are often delivered with a bit of an edge so you learned to retreat. You may have learned to think twice before asking for things you wanted. You may have become tentative about expressing your wishes. The well-intentioned shaping that is the mission of parents and teachers, too often left you unprepared for the adult world you were about to enter. You were taught to be less sure and less confident as a negotiator. By the time you became an adult, you had buried the wisdom you had when you were born and began buying books and going to seminars to "learn" things you once knew instinctively.

This book is designed to brush away those cobwebs, to get rid of the lies that have shaped your thinking, and to put you on the path to a successful negotiation, every time. It is designed to rid you of the fears that you have around negotiating so that you can return to being a fearless negotiator. I wrote this book to remind you how you can tap into the master negotiator that lives within you. Wish, Want, Walk is a simple method that lets you shed those old fears and falsehoods so that you will be all you can be in the negotiating room. The truth is that you can negotiate anything, right here, right now.

Take this book off your shelf before any important negotiation just to brush up on the concept. The nice thing is that once you understand the concept, you won't have any trouble remembering Wish, Want, Walk. You will carry it with you for as long as you are negotiating. It sticks in your brain like a good song and won't go away any time soon. Good luck!

FEAR is

False Evidence Appearing Real.

We all build up ideas in our head that just don't jibe with objective reality. I call these ideas false evidence. They seem real, but they aren't. There are a whole lot of things that fall into this category when it comes to negotiating. Believing the other person has all the power or believing that bad things will happen if you put your own desires on the table or believing that your world will come to an end if you walk away from a negotiation are all pieces of false evidence. Fear results when false evidence appears real to you. The reason this book was written was to give you a simple method to rid yourself of all those fears.

What Is a Negotiation?

In the early 1990s, for my first negotiating course at UCLA, I wrote my definition of a negotiation. It still holds up. My course has grown and changed over the years. My definition of a negotiation has not. A negotiation occurs anytime that:

- You ask someone to agree to something.
- You ask someone to do something.
- You just ask someone to get out of your way so you can do it yourself.

It is easy to forget life's myriad minor negotiations that go so smoothly that we forget they are indeed negotiations. You enter a restaurant and easily negotiate a different table from the one where they initially seated you. Or you get a cracked egg replaced at the check-out stand in the grocery store. Or you convince the cable company to give you a more specific time that the cable guy will show up at your house. Oh, you didn't win that one, huh? Well, we can't win them all. The point is that these every-day occurrences are all mini-negotiations. You hardly think about them or remember them, unless they turn ugly . . . or interesting.

What is absent from my definition of negotiation is whether the negotiation turns out to be win-win (meaning that each party comes out with much of what they want in the negotiation, which negotia-tions always ought to be) or I win-you lose (which can also be the case) or you win-I lose. What is also missing from my definition is any theoretical refer-ence to the style of the other side (is it positional or rational?) This book is not at all theoretical. It is about a simple method that works in any negotiation.

• Part 1 •

GETTING STARTED

Chapter 1

THE PLAN, PLAIN AND SIMPLE

THE WISH-WANT-WALK method has three simple steps: conjuring up your Wish result for this negotiation, understanding your Want (where you think the negotiation is most likely to end up in light of everything you know about the market and the person you are negotiating with), and setting your Walk Away point.

Your Wish is your dream result from the negotiation. This is the step that starts every negotiation, big or small. Someone somewhere wishes for something. That's how it all begins. So stop. Spend however much time it takes to make your Wish splendid. Let your imagination soar. This is a private activity. Do not edit yourself. Do not hold back. Wishing comes naturally to all human beings. We will explore ways to refine that most natural of all negotiating activities in Chapter 2.

Your Want is where the market forces most likely will drive the negotiation. This is the reality factor in any negotiation. We devote Chapter 3 to the things that drive the Want or the marketplace of the negotiation. If you have defined Want correctly, odds are, that is where the negotiation will finish. Thus, it is really important to get your Want right. There is nothing like knowing where you are most likely to end up in a negotiation. It makes the journey much easier.

Your Walk-Away point is just that. It is the line you draw in the sand—not in anger, not impulsively, not in the heat of the moment. You decide your Walk in advance with your teammates, whoever they are. It is the point at which you stop negotiating with a particular person on a particular issue and do something different to achieve your goals. You exercise your "or else." Knowing your Walk, along with thinking about it in advance, gives you strength and confidence. It is a single piece of information that gives you a great deal of power in a negotiation.

That is the Wish-Want-Walk method in a nutshell. If you have those three things well thought out, you are on your way to a successful negotiation. Having those three things firmly in mind before you start is like having your bags well packed for a trip. You start the trip with confidence that you have what you need and will not be surprised along the way.

Often people hear this summary of the plan and say, "Great. I will listen to what the other side has to say and then do just that. I will figure out my Wish, Want, Walk. Yes. I like that—Wish, Want, Walk. I'll do it as soon as I get back from my first negotiating session."

That is a natural reaction in these harried times when everybody seems to be in a rush. It's also a natural reaction of people who haven't used the Wish-Want-Walk method and thus haven't seen for themselves the benefits of proper planning. Waiting to see what the other side wants may seem to be a risk-free approach, but to get the most out of the negotiation, you should write down your Wish, Want, Walk before you sit down with the other side. If you wait to hear what the other side has to say before making your Wish-Want-Walk plan, you lose in three ways:

- You let the other side set the tone and define the playing field of the negotiation.

- You lose the ability to respond quickly, because you have a lot to think about.

- You lose the freedom to plan your future without being hampered by what you hear from the other side.

Let's do that another way. Here are the things you gain if set up your own Wish, Want, Walk before you meet with the other side:

- You get to define the negotiation.

- If you decide to go first, you get to plan exactly how to do that.

- You have time for everyone on your team to buy in to your Wish, Want, Walk, and that eliminates a lot of second-guessing.

Once you have your Wish, Want, Walk and have written these three points in a short memo to yourself, you will discover a whole new comfort zone as you commence the negotiation. In short, you will be able to manage a process that brings anxiety to many people. The next three chapters will help you set up your Wish, your Want, and your Walk. They present specific, guided ways to get ready for a negotiation. The method helps you by providing a format that you can keep for the rest of your life. You can use it as a quick reference for all your negotiations. Use the Wish-Want-Walk method to be sure that you have covered all the bases before going into any negotiation.

Wish, Want, Walk even goes on vacation with me. I had just finished facilitating a three-day intensive seminar in Singapore and was on a short flight to Sumatra to trek through the rain forests in the far north of that island. I wanted to see some wild orangutans in their natural habitat. My first negotiation upon arriving at the airport would be simple: arrange for a ride north until there was no more road. Then I would hike for an hour, keeping the river on my left until I reached a small settlement just inside the rain forest.

I used the price suggested in the Lonely Planet guidebook as my Want (where I expected the negotiation to end up if the car was in a relatively good condition). I set a Wish slightly cheaper, and I would Walk Away (literally) if there was more than a 10 percent increase in the price over my Want. I closed my eyes and enjoyed the rest of the flight as I conjured up images of the trip in my mind. I realized that part of my Wish, Want, Walk was a happy driver who would

Before you start
any negotiation,
set down your

Wish: Your Wish is your goal, your dream result.

Want: Your Want is where you think the negotiation
will end up according to external marketplace
forces. It is where the vast majority of deals
are closed.

Walk: Your Walk is the point at which you will walk
away from a deal because it is simply not
worth it. It is the point at which you lose
money or lose pride or lose status or feel
as though you lost and therefore won't do
the deal.

stop along the way for photographs. What a great way to start off this adventure!

When I arrived in Sumatra and cleared the small terminal, everything went exactly as planned even though I could not say "until the end of the road" in any of the several languages they speak. There is no taxi stand with meters at that airport. Instead, I worked through the English-speaking man in the parking lot whom I will call the Fixer. We started pretty far apart on price, so I switched over to the nonfinancial part of my Wish and settled on the driver (congenial, confident) and a relatively new SUV (the best of the bunch from what I could tell).

We went back to the money part of the deal and landed exactly on my Want. It helped that I kept waving the guidebook and pointing to the price and that I started to Walk Away several times. Indeed, if everything wasn't right, I was willing to find one of those wonderful buses filled with people and chickens and supplies and take my chances there. I was traveling with only a small day pack stuffed with ten days' worth of fresh underwear, T-shirts, and a shaving kit. Well, there was also a roll of toilet paper just in case.

I paid the agreed price to the Fixer and climbed up to the passenger seat, ready to be driven three hours to the edge of the rain forest. I had not understood a word of the complicated negotiation that involved dividing up my payment among the Fixer, the Driver, and the Disappointed Ones.

As the driver got in, I noticed a scowl on his face. I leaned forward with a big smile and said, "Hello." All people know a friendly greeting when they see one. He responded with a huge frown. He was definitely not happy. I jumped out of the car and called out to the Fixer, "This man is not happy. Why isn't he happy?"

"Don't worry, he is always like that."

"No, I saw him earlier. He was smiling when you told him where I wanted to go. It's a good haul, but he's not smiling now." The Fixer immediately went over and had a heated conversation with the Driver. This time I joined the two men as they haggled. I told the Fixer to give him more money. I could have cared less if the Fixer was happy. I wasn't going to spend the next three hours with him. He reluctantly complied. The surprised Driver talked some more to the Fixer. I said, "Give him more money."

"How much money do you think he should have?" There was an edge to the Fixer's sensible question.

"Until he is happy with the deal," was my simple answer. So the Fixer spoke very harshly to the Driver as he shoved more money in his hand. The Driver gave one of those forced grins that say, "I will smile, but I am still not happy." "More," I said sternly, and one more bill was peeled off. The Driver was so surprised that a big, spontaneous smile flashed across his face.

I got in, and off we went. He didn't speak any English beyond the very brief pleasantries we exchanged when first introduced, but we stopped at a rubber plantation, a grove of palms used for palm oil, and a roadside stand for a wonderfully refreshing drink of very fresh coconut milk. I shot several rolls of film. We were both happy because I had thought about my Wish, Want, Walk before we ever started the negotiation and it wasn't all about money. It rarely is.

This experience from my own life is typical. Know your Wish, Want, Walk ahead of time. Have a clear picture in your head. Wish, Want, Walk will guide you. But first you must carefully create those three items for your next negotiation.

For some people, creating a Wish, Want, Walk comes naturally. They like to spend a lot of time figuring things out before they start. Expending effort in this way is very comforting to them. Other people, by their very nature, like to jump into a project, letting it take them in whatever direction destiny dictates. They view preparation as hard work to be avoided at all costs. The majority of people fall somewhere in between. Be sure that you have someone on your team who likes to do the prep work. It is the bedrock of success in any negotiation.

- Be prepared.

- Look before you leap.

- Get ready, get set, go.

- The one with the most information wins.

- The better prepared you are, the better you will do.

Catchy phrases like these are limitless. Everyone has heard them. We all know they are true. But in our fast-paced world we are constantly cutting corners, and one of the first corners to be cut in negotiating is preparation. We never seem to have enough time to do the job right. Read the next three chapters. Take the time to work out your Wish, your Want, and your Walk before you do anything else. It is time well spent. Your negotiating path is much smoother. The results are more satisfying.

Chapter 2

MAKING WISHES

THE WISH IS YOUR GOAL—your dream result—the way you would have things turn out if you didn't have to negotiate with anyone, ask anyone's permission, or seek anyone's approval. It is the way the world would be if you controlled the world. This is the fun part. This is where you let your mind soar, your dreams take shape, and your hopes live as clearly and brightly as though they were today's reality.

The first step in setting your Wish is to take a look into your own perfect future. What is it that you would *love* to achieve in your life? How are your long-range goals affected by this negotiation? Do not edit yourself. Do not reject anything. You want to explore every possibility at this stage of the game. Whether you are by yourself on the beach or with a group of suits in the boardroom, be sure that all the ideas are given equal respect. Don't worry if some ideas engender a chuckle or two. This is where fearless negotiating begins. Don't let your mind conjure up an imaginary unpleasant reaction to your thoughts. Put words to your Wishes. Write them down.

If you don't begin by listing all your wishes, you run the risk that new ideas will keep popping into your head during the negotiating process. When this happens, you may feel torn and indecisive. The real problem is not indecision. The real problem is that you shortchanged yourself on preparing your Wish. You didn't start by listing all your possible—or even highly improbable—Wishes during your preparation. Have a freewheeling Wish session with yourself or with your entire team at the outset of the process. Leave no idea off the table in the initial round of brainstorming.

You should have fun with this step. It's like when you were a kid at your own birthday party and were told to close your eyes and make a wish. You didn't edit yourself then. Don't edit yourself now. Be fearless.

Whether you are alone or working with a group, what you will uncover in the process of creating your wish list is the true value of whatever is under negotiation, from your point of view. You might ask what does the phrase "true value" mean? You would be asking a very sophisticated question, and the answer to that question is a moving target. Think of anything you like, and I will quickly find ten people who will have ten different notions of its value. When I say "true value," I mean the value you personally place on something.

"Your true value" might be a better phrase than "true value" because what I am talking about is the value you (or your inner circle) place on goods and services before a negotiation starts and without regard to how the negotiation might turn out. Imagine Shakespeare's Richard III about to die on the battlefield saying, "A horse, a horse, my kingdom for a horse." He didn't ask people if they agreed or disagreed with his valuation. He meant what he said. Richard was in a pickle, and the only way out was a replacement for the horse he had just lost in battle. At that moment, in those circumstances, the true value of a horse to Richard III was huge—it was his entire kingdom.

Your true value for a specific item could change according to your perspective. For instance, if you owned an original oil painting by a famous artist and hired a professional appraiser to tell you its value, the first question the appraiser would ask would be the purpose of the appraisal. If you are selling, you will ask for and receive a somewhat higher appraisal. If you are buying, you will ask for and receive a somewhat lower appraisal. Your position in the world in relation to the item under discussion strongly affects where you set your true value. That is why the person you are negotiating with almost always will place a different value on something than you do. You are looking at the same thing from different perspectives.

If you were trying to insure the painting, you would ask for a high appraisal. But if you knew that the price of the premiums on the insurance policy was set by category of value on expensive paintings, you might want to reduce an appraisal that barely pushed you across some preset line into a higher category that would create a much higher premium. If you had that information, you might stay just under that line so that the insurance premium would be lower.

In your next negotiation, you are entitled to put any value you want on your product or service. Figuring out how to justify your Wish comes later. Right now you are making your Wish. You are deciding in your own mind, for your own purposes, exactly what value you are going to put on the goods or services you are buying or selling. If the item that is the subject of the negotiation is a commodity you are selling, you would typically compete primarily on price. In that case, you will have to look to reliability or delivery systems to create your value. True value starts in your mind. No one is going to value you and your services higher than you do.

Your idea of the true value of what you are negotiating is the key factor in setting your Wish. As a seller, you would never place your Wish below your notion of the true value of what it is you are offering. It is legitimate to hope to sell something for more than you think it is worth. Never open a negotiation to sell something by asking less than the true value you put on the item.

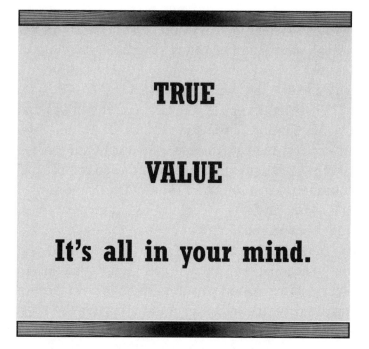

TRUE

VALUE

It's all in your mind.

Once you have drawn up your Wish list with all the wondrous possibilities you can dream up, you can begin culling the ideas down to a manageable group. If you have too many Wishes in any negotiation, you won't be able to focus your presentation—or your own thoughts, for that matter.

Culling the many wishes down to the final, more manageable number of goals is so important that I created a system to help you do that. In fact, I use the word *system* as an acronym (*s*pecific, *y*ou-centered, *s*tretch, *t*ime-sensitive, *e*verybody, *m*anageable) to guide you to your final Wish list.

First, get rid of the general ideas, the things that are not specific. If someone comes to you and says, "I am not happy," there is not much you can do about it. If someone says, "I want to go to Hawaii," you can take action. That is the Wish. To be part of the planning for a specific negotiation, your Wish must be specific.

Never lose sight of the main player in this and every negotiation you will ever have: you. *You*, of course, rarely means you alone as an individual with no need to answer to anybody. Even for the most personal purchase, you usually will include your spouse or partner. In a business environment, you may be part of a small company with perhaps only one or two other people who need to be included or may be part of a large company with a wide variety of people who need to be brought into the process. Whether the group is large or small, your Wish has to be centered on you, meaning the core group. You can't take a poll of people outside the core group to determine your goals and dreams. It is none of their business how high or low you set your sights. You (or your group) are the only one who matters in this process of setting goals. There are always folks out there who will discourage you and tell you that such and such is not possible. You don't need to hear from them. You and your inner circle just need to draw on your own experiences and values as you determine what you Wish to achieve.

Next, take anything off the list that is not a stretch for you. If you already have something in hand, it is not part of your Wish in the negotiation. It is part of your Want: what you expect out of the negotiation, where you think the marketplace will drive the negotiation. Everything on your Wish list should require you to stretch a bit.

Your Wish has to be time-sensitive. Some of your Wishes may be appropriate for a negotiation coming up on Monday. Others are Wishes that you have for the next few years, and so they need to be timed for the future. The less immediate Wishes may be mentioned in your initial presentation as things you want to accomplish in the future, not in the immediate negotiation. You let the other party know where you want to take the relationship. Of course, this does not apply to a one-time, price-only negotiation such as you might have on a used car lot or in a curio shop while on vacation. These are not the situations in which you discuss your long-range goals and aspirations unless they are part of your pitch for a better price. I am reminded of the young waiters who let you know they are saving for college. By letting you know their long-range Wish, they are hoping for an immediate improvement in the tip, which is their immediate Wish. They have time-coded their Wishes and used the long-range Wish to increase the chances that you will help them with the short-range Wish.

Be sure that everybody who needs to approve of your Wish list is brought into the process as soon as possible. Frequently, your organization will have a whole team of people who need to buy into the goals of the negotiation, that is, the Wishes that are being set. If you're smart, you will include some people who are not on the formal negotiating team but who can make your life miserable if they disagree with the result of your negotiation. Bring them aboard, perhaps in a less formal manner, but bring them aboard anyway. It will be worth your time in the long run to include everybody affected by the negotiation.

Finally, make sure that your Wishes are manageable in number. Maybe not now, maybe not tomorrow, but someday you will address all the items on your Wish list, so don't overload any single negotiation. Landing a man on the moon seemed impossible to a lot of Americans when the Wish initially was set. But those advising the president at that time were sure that it could be done given enough lead time, enough money, and a national commitment to do it. Sure enough, Neil Armstrong made the first footprint on the moon within the time set and only slightly over budget. Focusing on a single Wish turned out to be manageable.

To create workable Wishes,

be sure you use a SYSTEM:

S **Specific:** Your Wish must be specific or you won't know when you have achieved it.

Y **You-centered:** These are your (or your company's) hopes, dreams, and aspirations. You and your core group must base your goals on the values and ambitions you hold dear—no one else's.

S **Stretch:** A Wish that is not worth the reach doesn't deserve the name. Make sure your Wishes make you stretch at least a little.

T **Time-sensitive:** There is a tide and time to everything, even your dreams. Peg a time to each item on your Wish list. That will help you know how to present your Wish when you make the opening offer.

E **Everybody:** Be sure you have buy-in from the entire team and even from the people who will bug you about it later.

M **Manageable:** Don't overwhelm the negotiation with too many Wishes. The more focused you are, the more likely you are to achieve your dreams.

In a class that I was teaching at a prestigious institution recently, one participant felt that a professor who taught at the college he was attending had mistreated him. The student had taken his case to the provost, and after a six-month "investigation" he was told that the professor has been "talked to" and the incident had been handled. The student said that what he really wanted was to have the professor publicly slapped. Inside, I was saying, "Are you crazy?" Silently, without reaction, I wrote that on the flipchart without comment.

The group adopted the student's renegotiation with school authorities as a class project. They used the SYSTEM to come up with a Wish list. A public slapping was not on the final list of Wishes. Its presence on the flipchart, however, shaped the entire conversation because it underscored the emotional intensity that a few members of the group felt toward the subject of the negotiation.

How did it turn out? The professor apologized to the student. A memorandum about his behavior was put in his personnel file, and he was counseled.

Joyfully, these three results were three of the items placed on the Wish list that the students put together as a homework assignment. Let's test this scenario against the SYSTEM for creating a Wish list. The three Wishes were specific and were "you-centered" in that they were what the students wanted, not what anyone else wanted. The three Wishes were a bit of a stretch and were very time-sensitive since graduation was just weeks away. Everybody agreed to those Wishes, and they were manageable in number. Everybody was happy with the result, especially the student who initially felt wronged by the incident. A large part of the aggrieved student's happiness was based on the fact that his far-out Wishes were included on the initial list. He was less frustrated because he got to verbalize his Wish and it was treated with respect. He felt heard for the first time in the process. This experience reinforced for me the importance of listening to every suggestion for the wish list and to place every suggestion on the list even when you don't agree with them. The group will weed out the bad ideas as they apply the SYSTEM to the initial group of ideas that are listed. Ultimately, the complaining student was the one who eliminated the outlandish Wishes.

Learn More about Yourself

As you think about your Wish, you realize how intensely personal it is. If you don't know who you are and where you want to go, you have no clear way to establish your short- or long-range goals, no matter how much you know about what you are negotiating or about the other person.

Learn all you can about yourself. Learn about your personality type, set out your vision of your future, and understand realistically where you fit into your organization. Sometimes I speak and teach about the benefits of a three-year plan for everybody.

In your business you should also have a written three-year plan so that everybody who works with you will know where the business is going. Everyone in the office should be familiar with the plan. In fact, you should know as much as you can about the entire team. If you are an agent or a lawyer negotiating on behalf of someone else as the principal, you need to know all you can about the person for whom you are negotiating. Ask that person what his or her three-year plan is. What picture does that person have in his or her head of life in three years? How does that person see his or her life in three years? The picture in that person's head almost always affects the current negotiation directly.

In your personal life, you also need a three-year plan. Whether it is written or not, you should have a vision—a picture in your head—of what life will be like in three years. That way, your negotiations can feed your vision. The actions you take, the places you invest your time, the books you read—everything you do—moves you either toward your vision or away from your vision. Create your vision right now. When you know all that, you will be on your way to becoming a world-class negotiator.

What Negotiating Style to Use

This book is not designed to change your negotiating style, which is exactly what many people think is the key to success as a negotiator: "I want to be more assertive." "I want to laugh less." "I want to be more serious in a negotiation." "I want to learn how to intimidate people exactly the way I have been intimidated. I want them to know how it feels." These are all comments that I hear at the beginning of seminars when we go around the room to find out why people came to the course and what they want to get out of it.

Many participants want to be more like the person who beat up on them in the last negotiation. If they were yelled at, they want to learn to yell back. If they were outtalked by a loquacious charmer, they want to learn to tell stories that are even better.

World-class negotiators come in all sizes, shapes, colors, and personality types. There is no single style that must be used if you are to get what you want in life. Successful negotiators, like successful people in general, are individuals who let their light shine forth, no matter what it is.

Mrs. Brooke Astor, the New York socialite, was caught up in one of the toughest negotiations of all. When she was in her nineties, a mugger approached her on the streets of New York, demanding that she turn over her purse and jewels. Always proper, she said, "I'm sorry. I don't think we have been properly introduced. I am Mrs. Brooke Astor."

She stood politely and firmly waiting for a proper response. The mugger ran off.

Trust your own style. It is where you are most comfortable, and most likely to find success in a negotiation. Sticking with your own style increases the odds of success in a negotiation enormously because you will appear more genuine and therefore more trustworthy. You are not trying to be someone you are not.

As a young lawyer, I was dazzled (maybe slightly jealous) and in awe of my kid sister, Sally, who was rising rapidly in the financial world. Even though she was a high school dropout, she became president of a wholly owned subsidiary of Penn Mutual Life Insurance Company without ever lying about her education. When she was vice president at Oppenheimer, she had twenty-one MBAs reporting to her.

She would call me about once a week. This was in the old days before the electronic answering systems that are omnipresent today. I would hear "It's your sister Sally" over the intercom. I would pick up the phone, and she would tell a joke, straight out, without a "Hi," "It's me," or "How are you?" The jokes were always funny, and while I was laughing, she would hang up. That was it. For several years, my relationship with my sister centered on those wonderful phone calls. My other sister would keep me up on what was going on with Sally's meteoric rise.

I decided that Sally's success was due to her great facility to remember and tell jokes, and so I started writing the jokes down. I learned them. I rehearsed them. I told them in meetings.

I am not a joke teller. The jokes bombed.

I could stop any meeting, anywhere, any time by retelling one of my sister's jokes. It was not pretty.

I learned that what worked for Sally would not work for me. It took me many more years to learn that the best style was my own style. If I wanted to be a world-class negotiator, I had to believe in myself. I had to use the unique person who was me. If I tried to be anybody else, it would not work.

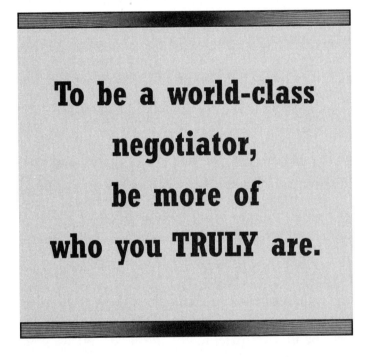

Who Do You Want to Serve?

One of the most important things you have to decide about yourself is what kind of business you want and what kind of customers you want to serve. Once you have thought about that, you can decide which customers are apples—to be polished regularly—and which are onions—to be discarded before they make you cry. You will increase your job satisfaction substantially by thinking about the sorts of persons you will allow into your business family as clients, customers, and vendors. Unfortunately, sometimes you will have to learn the hard way what types fit into your business life. We all accept clients and customers we wish we had not accepted.

The apple and onion images have helped me—and a lot of other people—think about how to sort through this issue of who is and who is not a desirable addition to one's business and personal lives. I have even constructed a matrix so that you will have a graphic to help you think about how to use this metaphor. Figure 2-1 shows an apple in the upper right-hand box to represent the folks you want to seek out and welcome into your business life. Those people have a lot of the qualities you like to work with. The figure shows an onion in the lower left-hand box to represent the folks you don't want in any part of your life, personal or professional. These people have few qualities you like and one or more qualities you don't enjoy and don't want to have in your business life.

You will notice that there are two small boxes below the onion and below the apple. These boxes are there for you to write down the qualities that make a person an onion for you and the qualities that make a person an apple for you

Figure 2-1

Fill in the two boxes under the apple. Each box is a quality you like to see in your customers. Think about the best client or customer you ever had. Decide on two words that represent that client's behavior. Write one word in each of the boxes.

Now fill in the two boxes under the onion. Each box is a quality you do not like to see in your cus-

tomers. Think about the worst pain-in-the-neck customer you ever had. Decide on two words that represent that client's behavior. Write one word in each
of the boxes.

For me, the boxes under the apple would be
"understanding " and "appreciation." By "understanding" I mean that it is very important that my
clients get what I do for them and know how what I
do benefits them. If they do not, the work still gets
done, but the psychic payoff is missing. Like most
people, I feel that job satisfaction is important.
Appreciation manifests itself in being responsive
when we need some information and paying bills on
time. The boxes under the onion would be "worrisome" and "unappreciative." By "worrisome," I
mean clients who are so nervous about how a deal is
going to turn out that they call repeatedly with the
same questions. "Unappreciative" clients don't
understand the effort we have to expend and seem to
take a favorable result for granted. Sometimes they
are short with my team members who are trying to
help them. This usually manifests itself in a failure to
be responsive when we need something from them
and a failure to stay current in their payments. For
me, the apples are the clients with a high return to
my psyche and my pocketbook (understanding and
appreciative) and the onions are clients with a low
return to my psyche and my pocketbook (worrisome
and unappreciative).

The two words that you put in the boxes will be
different—maybe very different from anyone else's—
but these are questions you must think about regularly. One person's apple is another person's onion.

Who are the apples and who are the onions for you and your business? Be rigorous about this even if you don't think you can obtain many apples. You must know what sorts of people you want to serve.

Let's be realistic. You will never turn an onion into an apple. It is not possible. But you can look at the unpleasant aspects of a person's personality or conduct and change something you have control over. For me, it is often simply a matter of charging more.

At least those people will become highly profitable onions. You're more willing to tolerate them if they pay well, but an onion is still an onion. More often I say to myself that life's too short. The better choice is to work only for apples you know while you try to add others. In a world of abundance, you fire your onions, make room, and add apples. Sometimes if my contact person within a company is an onion, I try to change my contact person. This is a delicate political dance, but I have pulled it off more than once. If it works, I have an apple to deal with without losing the business.

If I can't do anything to improve the relationship with the client, I will call the client into my office and explain how important it is for him or her to have a lawyer that he or she feels close to and really wants to work with and will suggest two or three young lawyers, all of whom charge a good deal less, and urge the client to interview and select another lawyer. One of two things happens: This conversation amounts to a wake-up call and I receive the desired behavior change or the client leaves, which is fine.

Now figure out how you can have more apples. One of the most important steps is to stay away from the onions. You can spot them. Tag them and turn them down. Smile all the way home. When you turn down an onion, you win twice:

1. You don't have to deal with that person.

2. One of your competitors does.

When you have a client or customer who is an onion, figure out what changes can make the relationship less painful. I have mentioned the two techniques I use most often. Think about how you can move your onions into one of the empty squares in the illustration. They won't be apples, but they won't be raw onions either.

Don't be afraid to jettison the onions altogether. Many people working for large corporations are reluctant to get rid of onions because most of the pain will fall on other employees and the presence of the income the onions bring to the balance sheet may help them in some way. In small businesses, there is often a fear of dumping the onions because of lessened cash flow. The opposite is true. Your income will go up when you are working only for apples. You will enjoy your work more and be more productive. Apples by definition appreciate your efforts and reward you appropriately.

Chapter 3

UNDERSTANDING WANT

THE NEXT ELEMENT IN THE Wish-Want-Walk method is to understand Want. Your Want is the place where you think the negotiation is most likely to end up on the basis of all the facts and circumstances in the situation. Let's face it, most often the negotiation is going to end up where the marketplace dictates. No matter who is negotiating the deal, no matter how blustery someone becomes, no matter how much rehearsal goes on, the market is king. The market rules. The marketplace (your Want) is the single most stabilizing factor in a negotiation. Because Want is really a marketplace projection, it is more akin to a target than to a specific number, although I like the discipline of using a single number when I set up Wish, Want, Walk for any negotiation. Setting a specific number as opposed to a range requires you to focus your attention.

Anybody who knows the market well knows the approximate amount that something will sell for or something can be purchased for. Price is often the easiest part of the negotiation. It is all the other things you and your customer want that make the negotiation interesting. It is all the other things that will push the price up or down—things such as delivery, quality, scope of work, other services, exclusivity, experience, and customer service. Each one of those things should have its own Wish, Want, Walk.

The best source of information about the marketplace is your own experience, but there are lots of other sources. As seminars turn to this subject, I always ask where the participants go for their information about market conditions. Younger audiences shout out, "The Internet!" Older members of the audience more often start with their friends and contacts in the industry.

Cost, Price, and Value

To understand Want, you must understand the differences among cost, price, and value. When you understand these three distinct concepts, you will gain powerful insight into the role of the marketplace in establishing your Want. In seminars, we introduce this trichotomy by asking, "What does value mean?" A lot of people answer, "It's the cost of something" or "It's the price of something." The true value of something is very different.

The true value of something is whatever you say it is for you. Someone else probably will place a different value on the same item. Never does one figure represent the value of an item at all times, in all places, and to all people. We talked a lot about true value in Chapter 2. Even gold fluctuates in its price, so we say the value of gold fluctuates. The dollar fluctuates in the price that citizens of other countries pay for it, so we say the value of the dollar is rising or falling. Retail goods lose value over time; that is why there are sales.

The price of something is what people end up paying in the marketplace. It is the number written on the price tag. When you think you got a real bargain, you are saying that you put a value on something that was higher than the price you paid for that item. The price of similar items sold at the same time in the same general area tends to be about the same no matter who you buy them from. You can bargain the price down a bit, but the price tends to stay within a range set by the marketplace. Projecting the price you are most likely to pay for something is what this chapter is all about.

The cost is what is spent getting a product to market: raw materials, manufacturing, packaging, and shipping plus some overhead and some profit. Cost is all the money it takes to put a piece of merchandise in a customer's hand.

In fact, value, price, and cost are another way of defining the Wish (your idea of the true *value* of an item), the Want (the marketplace *price* of an item), and the Walk (the *cost* to create the item, including some profit).

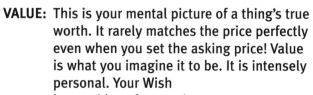

VALUE: This is your mental picture of a thing's true worth. It rarely matches the price perfectly even when you set the asking price! Value is what you imagine it to be. It is intensely personal. Your Wish is your idea of true value.

PRICE: This is the number at which things are bought and sold in the marketplace. It fluctuates over time and varies in different locales. It is your Want.

COST: This is the expense to create the product and get it in the customer's hand. Cost (plus some overhead and some profit) usually defines the Walk Away for the seller.

The Three Kings
of Commerce

As you decide the market value of whatever you are selling, keep in mind the three kings of commerce. There are three aspects that make up the price of every product and service. The ideal customer understands that if the price is to be reasonable, the other two elements have to be reasonable (see Figure 3-1).

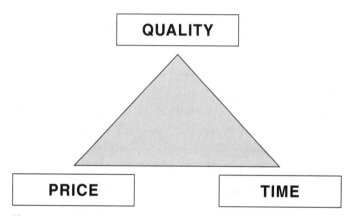

Figure 3-1

If a customer comes in with a rush job, that is going to pull the triangle out of balance. Either the price will have to go up or the quality is going to suffer. That rule of commerce is as predictable and reliable as any rule of physics. It is a rule of life. Throw the balance off in any one direction and adjustments will occur in one or both of the other directions.

If a customer wants higher quality, the price will rise and it probably will take a little longer. Be sure you understand what limitations you have as far as customer demands are concerned. Plan ahead for requests that make the price go up. That way, when the customer asks for faster delivery or better quality, you can answer by describing the effect that request has on the price. When customers ask for a lower price, you can let them know the impact on quality or delivery time. In our office, quality will not be forsaken, so any rush increases the price. Any price reduction will increase the time to deliver.

Price and Time

The way time pushes and pulls on price merits some special discussion. Goods delivered quickly almost always cost more, especially if the goods are specially built items that must be assembled and delivered quickly. Whether you are building a house, putting together a computer, or rushing out a print job, there is an added charge for meeting a deadline that is shorter than the norm.

What isn't so obvious to a lot of people is the way certain services—especially professional services such as consulting, accounting, law, engineering, and design work—are affected by time. Your early conversations and first efforts on behalf of a client are often the most valuable. The more intangibles that are involved, the truer the statement is, but it is true even if you are selling widgets to a supplier who bases his or her decisions almost entirely on price. Ironically, it can be difficult to charge adequately for such initial advice and planning.

Figure 3-2 shows what I mean.

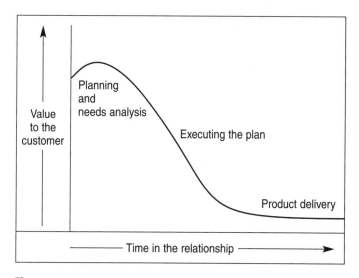

Figure 3-2

The final delivery of a tangible product is the point in the relationship where there is the least value and the greatest chance for complaints. The early work of assessing needs is the most valuable and the most insulated from criticism. After all, everybody has a right to his or her opinion. Most often, it is at the initial stage where the highest value to the client or customer lies. You need to figure out how to charge for it.

As a young lawyer trying to build a practice, I had a policy of providing an initial one-hour free consultation to independent filmmakers. I viewed it as a way to help the embryonic independent filmmaking community of which I wanted to be a part. The filmmakers were always appreciative and often would call back with a follow-up question or two and maybe call back again. I found it difficult to cut that off, at least before the contracts had to be drawn, but there was always somebody else who could produce the contracts less expensively. Once I had developed a strategy and laid out a plan of work in the initial meeting, the potential client usually could find another lawyer to execute the plan more cheaply than I would. Now I charge a consultation fee. Not only does it represent a nice bit of income, it weeds out nonserious filmmakers. It eliminates the non-payers and strongly inhibits the time-consuming follow-up questions that seem to know no boundaries. My practice has flourished since I began to charge for the initial planning and strategy work I do for new clients. The big picture is usually my most valuable contribution to the client.

Scouting the Opposition

In addition to researching generalized information about the price the marketplace puts on the thing you are selling or buying, you want to determine the value of the thing you are negotiating to the individual on the opposite side of the table. For instance, after you have established a fair market value for something you are selling, say, your business, you want to adjust your Want up or down depending on the buyer. If the potential buyer of your business is a venture capital company looking for a bargain, the Want—the most likely result of the negotiation—

will probably be a little lower than your "fair market" appraisal. If the buyer is a competitor who needs some patents you hold or needs customers you have or needs a sales team you have built, the value will be higher to that person, so the price will go up.

A critical driver to the place where the negotiation is going to end up is the party on the other side of the table. That seems obvious, yet the biggest single mistake people make when they negotiate is not to learn all they can about the person with whom they are negotiating.

John Friess, the vice president of wired.MD, Inc., realizes how important it is to know everything you can about the person with whom you are negotiating. His company creates high-quality educational videos for healthcare providers to show their patients to reinforce what they tell a patient in the hospital or clinic. The product reduces the misunderstandings that often trigger errors in the follow-up that needs to happen after the doctor visit.

Another company that sells similar products to public libraries offered to license copies of 70 of the videos wired.MD had created. It would place the videos of wired.MD with over 600 new customers. It offered to pay a royalty with a minimum guarantee of $105,000 over a three year period—a lot of money to wired.MD. The price per unit was low, but wired.MD could have used the money, and besides, it had only sold to one library customer in the past.

Shortly after a seminar in which we stressed the importance of gathering information about the opposition, John jumped into the process and started digging for more information about the buyer. He pressed to find out exactly who the 600 customers were. He found out that the buyer counted an entire system of libraries as a single customer. Some state library systems can have up to 1,500 libraries as one customer. Multiply this by the 600 new customers and you can see that the high-quality videos that normally sold for a $195 apiece would have been sold at a fire sale price. The buyer didn't care because it made its money bulkling up content. The fact that the content was high-quality was just a happy accident.

As soon as it found out how the buyer defined the word *customer*, wired.MD Walked Away from the deal. The last thing it wanted to do was cheapen its product with this scheme, although the money would have helped its balance sheet. By making a concerted effort early in the game, wired.MD saved its sales resources and its relationship with the buyer.

There is a whole laundry list of things you might want to know about the other person. Make your own list for each negotiation. Here are the most important things you want to know about the other person:

- What is your best, most informed estimate of the person's Wish, Want, Walk?

- What is the other person's authority?

- Who is the other person's client?

Believe it or not, every one of these questions can be answered before you lay eyes on the person with whom you will be negotiating. How do you begin to find out? First, use the Internet and colleagues in the industry and trade journals for the industry to find out as much as you can about your opposite number. What are his or her interests, and what is his or her ability to close the deal without checking with anybody else? All this and more can be uncovered with a little detective work. You also can ask people in companies that recently have done similar deals with your opposite number. People usually are willing to open up once they know you are listening to what they have to say.

Sometimes all your efforts don't turn up much information, but many times over the years I have received some of the hottest tips from cold calls to perfect strangers. Use easygoing but probing questions to extract as much information as you can about the person who will be sitting across the table from you, including that person's Wish, Want, Walk and authority to close the deal and who that person's client is.

Let me explain about the "client." Everyone has to answer to someone, usually several someones. You are not the only person in the negotiation with myriad pressures from myriad persons. The more you know about the pressures and problems in the life of the person across the table, the better off you will be.

Without that information, you will be in a constant battle with unnamed ghosts, with powerful forces unseen and unknown, with factors you cannot influence because you do not know their nature or name.

Do not accept the obvious. In my field, I routinely negotiate with agents and managers. It would be easy to assume that the client is the person they are representing. With junior talent agents, the client is not so much the nominal actor or director or writer they are representing as it is their bosses in the agency. Promotions within the agency may be more important to a junior agent than a client to whom the agent can explain almost anything. The agent can always convince the nominal client that a deal is good or bad or that a deal needs to be accepted or not. It is the immediate supervisor of the agent whom the agent wants to impress. In such a situation, you need to find out all you can about the supervisor because the supervisor is the real client being served by the agent.

Here are some other things you might want to know: What are the hobbies of the other persons? What is their family situation? What is their budget if you are selling something? What does the deal mean to them within their organization? What is their character and reputation? What is of value to them? What are their plans for the future?

You are always negotiating with a person. You are never negotiating with GE or Universal Studios or Macy's. The individual negotiator from GE (or Universal Studios or Macy's department store) may hide behind those mighty edifices, but that person is a human being with his or her own hopes and dreams and fears and foibles. Get to know that person and you will be much farther ahead in your negotiation.

Risk and Reward

Another element that pulls and pushes on the price of many transactions is how much risk you are willing to take. Some people are gamblers, and some are not. Companies reflect their leader and his or her appetite for risk. That is why some companies are gamblers and some are not. This basic premise should always be in the back of your mind when you negotiate.

Like the three kings of commerce, the tension between risk and reward is fundamental in any negotiation. The higher the risk, the higher the potential for reward. This is the ancient rule of risk and reward. The rewards go to those who take the risks. This has been true throughout the world and down through time.

> If you want to share in the gain
> You have to share in the pain.
> If your focus is to avoid pain,
> You are going to sacrifice gain.

This risk-reward notion pushes the final price of an item up and down between the cost of the item and its value in the minds of the parties to the negotiation. This is particularly true for large items or specially built items such as factories, dams, airplanes, and custom homes. Take the niggling notion of a markup. Let's say you want to mark up the cost of subcontractors or mark up other costs you might incur before you send the bill for those goods or services to the client. What is the justification for the markup?

When you order goods and services and pass them on to the client, you are taking certain risks in addition to the administrative cost of supplying the goods and services. Depending on the business, here are a few of those risks:

1. Can the subcontractor perform?

2. Can the subcontractor deliver on time?

3. Is the subcontractor financially healthy?

4. Is the subcontractor safe?

5. Does the subcontractor understand schedule?

6. Will the subcontractor follow procedures?

When you take risks such as these, you deserve a reward.

There are a lot of other risks that the other side may want you to take. They may want you to take the risk that weather will hold things up. In an international transaction, they may want you to take the risk of currency fluctuation. In big companies, there is often a risk management team. In small companies, the owner typically relies on his or her gut feeling to determine how much risk to accept. No matter what type of risk you are assuming, always be sure to negotiate some reward for yourself for taking on that risk.

Chapter 4

YOUR WALK-AWAY POINT AND POWER— REAL POWER

NOW WE ARRIVE AT THE PART OF THE Wish-Want-Walk method that gives you real power no matter who you are or who you are up against. Your Walk Away point is just that: the point at which you bow out of the negotiation you are in and move on. Be sure to establish your Walk Away point before you walk into the negotiating room.

Establishing a Walk-Away point early in the process runs against human nature. Most people do not want to start preparing for a negotiation by thinking about the possibility that the negotiation might not succeed, that they might not get what they want. But in fact, that is one of the first things you should do. It will put real power behind your position.

Having a well-defined Walk-Away point levels the playing field no matter how unbalanced the bargaining power may appear to an outsider. The reason is simple: The other side would not be in the room with you unless you had something they wanted. They may want it a little or they may want it a lot, but they want it or they wouldn't be there. With your Walk Away point defined, you have decided before you start the negotiation that you will not give up the things they want unless they make it worth your while and you have decided exactly what that means. They can yell and scream and threaten and cajole, but they are not getting what they want unless they meet a certain threshold price. That's power.

Fortunately, most negotiations are settled in the Want area. However, the tough ones may move closer to your Walk-Away point. This is not a comfortable area. When you find yourself in that area without a Walk-Away position ahead of time, you flounder, you panic, and indecision sets in. With a Walk-Away point, you know it is time to try to change focus, make concessions in other areas, or adjust something, such as quality or delivery schedule or payment terms, that makes up for some of the demands that are being put on you. But do not pass your Walk Away point just because you are under that momentary pressure.

Let's look at some examples that will help you get a grip on how to set up your Walk-Away point. The most common Walk-Away point in business is a number: "If we don't get $X, we're walking away." The Walk-Away number is generally the cost of goods plus the overhead that is applied to the product plus some profit. There has to be profit in every transaction. This approach to establishing your Walk number is more relevant or less relevant depending on the business you are in. If you are in a commodity business, price is the real driver, with delivery and sometimes even quality taking a backseat. If you are in a value-based business such as software, consulting, or screenwriting, the cost of goods has little application. If Microsoft software were priced on the basis of cost plus overhead plus 10 percent profit, it would sell for a lot less.

In negotiating salary at a firm or business where you have been working for several years, you should know the range of your increase because you have knowledge gathered over time before your review. If that is the case, the focus of your Walk might be something like having your own assistant. The Walk doesn't have to be a number, although you better know the cost of anything on your list even if it does not involve dollars to you. In this example, the salary of the assistant, the cost of the fringes, and the assistant's desk are all parts of the cost to your company.

Although there are certain financial imperatives that drive the Walk position, the more important elements are things that you alone can decide. They involve your self-pride and self-image. If you just wouldn't feel good about accepting a salary lower than $X, so be it. Think about it. Look at whether it is reasonable. But if your soul needs $X per week, that is your Walk number no matter what others think. Someone in your life may think that your Walk number should be higher. However, if you would feel bad about missing out on an opportunity by setting the bar that high, don't do it no matter how sound the advice seems. Your Walk is your personal choice.

The good news is that setting up your Walk-Away point is not as difficult as it sounds. There are three simple steps to the process:

Step 1 in creating a Walk-Away point is to know that you have choices. Some people are born with this optimistic attitude. Other people always seem worried about the future of their business and the outcome of any negotiation. The universe is a great storehouse of unlimited opportunity. There are more customers in the world for your product or service than you could ever meet, let alone sell to. Know that you have choices. Make that your mantra.

Step 2 in establishing your Walk-Away point is to think about what those choices are. It is one thing to have a general view of abundance about the world around you; it is another thing to have a specific list of choices in the negotiation you are about to enter. Make a list of choices that you have in the real world if this negotiation does not work. That is, you should know exactly what you will do if things don't work out with the person you are currently up against. As you make your list of choices, your power should become clear to you.

Step 3 is to look over the list and pick your "or else." Since I started practicing entertainment law, I have had the occasional client who would say, "I won't do this for a penny less than $X." My response, even before I started thinking critically about negotiating, was always "What is your 'or else'?" I then would explain that life is always about choices. When you say you are going to walk away from a situation, know exactly where it is that you are going to go. Know your "or else."

This concept is the core of the negotiating course taught at Harvard University. There they use the label BATNA, which is an acronym for *best alternative to a negotiated agreement*. They teach—as I do—that you should never start a negotiation until you have determined your "or else," the choice you will exercise if things don't work out in this negotiation.

Knowing ahead of time what will send you out of the room greatly increases the odds that it will never happen. There will be no invisible lines crossed, because, to you, at least, the lines will be very visible. Before you reach the Walk-Away point, you send all sorts of signals to the other side: "I really don't have any more room here" or "I can't give much more here." You have an automatic built-in resistance point just above your pre-set Walk-Away point. You put on the brakes. You begin making smaller concessions and giving them greater thought.

The single most effective thing
you can do to create power
in your position and project power
in your presentation
is to establish your

WALK-AWAY POINT.

If you know that you will walk away
if you have to, it will affect
the way you enter the room
and everything you say
after you get there.

Knowing your Walk-Away point ahead of time prevents the worst result. That's when you make a deal and realize later that it is unacceptable. You indulged yourself in the moment of the negotiation without considering your Walk-Away point. "Buyer's remorse" can feel like a giant hangover. What a terrible thing it is. It leads to depression, poor self-esteem, loss of hair, and sometimes loss of job. You don't want to experience that one if you can avoid it, and you can. It is all up to you. Set your Walk before you start negotiating. It is as important to set your Walk before the negotiation as it is to set your Wish and your Want.

Keep in mind that determining your Walk includes determining in advance what you will do if this negotiation does not work out—what your "or else" is. It doesn't always mean physically walking out of a negotiation. Sometimes that is simply not possible.

Ray Rapko is a consultant who deals with this reality frequently. He is a Sarbanes-Oxley internal auditor. Sarbanes-Oxley is the name of the federal legislation that was passed after the Enron scandal to clean up corporate accounting and disclosure. His role is to help companies by performing an internal audit to ensure that the financial controls are in place to comply with Sarbanes-Oxley. For him to do his job, he needs to gather a lot of information from various people in middle management. They are usually overworked, underpaid, stressed out, and certainly not needing more things to do, such as rounding up a bunch of information. It should come as no surprise that people are not enthusiastic about the exercise and often fail to cooperate with Ray and give him what he needs, in the time he needs it.

Ray certainly can't walk away. He can't force the other person to walk away by firing that person. His "or else" has to be something else. His Walk Away comes when he asks for a piece of information and he realizes he won't receive it in time to meet his deadline. That is when he issues a warning that if he doesn't hear back by the next day, he will have to go to the boss. That usually works, but if he doesn't receive the needed information, he moves up the chain of command until he does.

Even though Ray is in a situation where he can't literally Walk Away, he has set his Walk and follows through on it. He can do that nicely, consistently, and without creating much upset because he has thought about his Wish, Want, Walk in advance and has it organized in his mind. He knows what he is going to do and can do it without a lot of drama even though the situation is one that could lead to a lot of whining, raised voices, or a confrontation of some sort.

Once you establish your Walk-Away position, you need to honor it. Don't change it because a good customer gives you a hard time about it. That is why you set it in the first place: You decide ahead of time when you will walk instead of having to decide on the spot with an important client staring you down. Honor your preset Walk-Away point.

You are much more likely to honor your Walk-Away Point when you write it down beforehand. You still can change your Walk based on new information, but you will do it consciously instead of letting the negotiation slip off the mark in reaction to the situation. If you do not write down your Walk Away ahead of time, it is easy to forget exactly what it was. Thankfully, most negotiations do not get close to the Walk-Away point. When they do, it is only after you have been negotiating for a while, and so your Walk Away can get crossed before you realize it. The truth is that you lose track of your Walk Away because it wasn't set out in writing. All you can say is "yikes" and begin backpedaling like crazy.

Another way to make it easier to enforce your Walk is to share it. You will create some peer pressure on yourself to hold the line.

The very best thing you can do to help you enforce your Walk-Away point is to be sure that your boss agrees with it. If you don't have a boss on this particular negotiation, be sure that you have agreement from whoever it is you will be answering to after the negotiation is over. Maybe it is a spouse, or maybe it is a partner. Whoever it is you will go to with the results of the negotiation, be sure to have an agreement on your Wish and your Want and your Walk before you get started.

Of course, if you gain some new information about a key consideration such as your costs, you can adjust your Walk. That has nothing to do with the pressure from your client. It has to do with your costs and what you need to keep your business going. Or maybe you will get a call from the manufacturing guys, who have figured out a way to meet delivery requests that did not seem possible when the process started. Then the Walk can be changed. If client pressure makes you come up with a creative solution, that is good. If client pressure causes you to cave in on your Walk for no good reason except the threat of their leaving, that is bad.

When the pressure builds, you instinctively, but dangerously, start looking at your Walk position. Exercise great caution here. It is a good thing to look at your Walk position and your Want and your Wish. However, if your Walk position was well formulated ahead of time, it is the position least likely to be modified after the negotiation begins.

If the demands of the other side take you below the Walk-Away point, you will have to Walk Away from this deal even if you thought you couldn't afford to lose it at the beginning of the negotiation. No matter how unlikely it is that those circumstances will come up, they do. And when they do, you have to walk away. You simply cannot accept some deals if you intend to stay in business.

You might be saying, "Why would I want to think about walking away at all? Sometimes I can't walk away. Sometimes I have a customer who digs in her heels and I can't afford to lose the customer. I have to go along. I can't lose that customer."

A big customer or two may mean a great deal to your business even though those customers drive a hard bargain. Sometimes those customers feel like a 400-pound gorilla when you are negotiating with them. It may be true that to lose such a customer would be really tough on a short-term basis. The lesson for me and for you and for everybody who operates a small business is that when you lose a very important customer or client, the universe moves in to fill that big hole. I had to learn this lesson the hard way. In fact, it was one of the toughest lessons I ever learned. The year was 1991. I had been practicing law for over twenty years, and my practice included some of my lifelong heroes. In fact, my legal work for Michael Landon, who starred in or produced many television series, including *Little House on the Prairie*, made up about half of my practice. The business was going great. I was healthy. My personal life was the best. In fact, I was preparing to go on a month long trip to Asia. Life was sweet.

Then I got a call one afternoon at the office that I remember to this day. It was Michael's producer calling in on the private line he and Michael always used. "Michael," he said with a slight questioning rise to the word. "Yeah, what's up?" was my standard response.

"Michael has cancer of the pancreas." I was stunned.

"It's inoperable." I couldn't speak.

"He only has a month or two, three at the most." Silence.

"You better come out to the house."

The fog didn't lift for days. We all did what we had to do for Michael and his family. Michael passed away before my trip, but when I came back, the practice of law was forever changed for me. The television portion of my practice was nearly nill. The independent film side of my practice flourished.

I hope you never have to go through the loss of a friend, hero, or major client as I did. Years later, I still feel the loss of Michael Landon's wonderful presence in my life. But I did learn that on a business level, there are always other opportunities. No matter how important a client or customer is to you, you can always regroup and go forth in prosperity.

I now maintain my practice so that no one is responsible for that large a portion of my business. Even half that share would be too much today. No single client accounts for over 10 percent of our revenues. You should try to always keep a diverse list of clients so that no one of them becomes someone you cannot afford to lose.

When someone starts becoming a dominant supplier or a dominant customer, that is the time to start planning for expansion or for that person's departure so that you don't have the awful feeling that you are the captive of that person's business. If you start to believe that you can't afford to lose a certain customer, refocus your thinking. Such a loss is most definitely a possibility. Make the adjustments necessary to reduce the pain of that loss by expanding your business.

I have a friend who works for a large international firm. His sole job is to negotiate deals that have gone sour for one reason or another. He liked this section of the book and agreed in general but wrote, "If you're Boeing and selling military aircraft and the client has received your product but is unhappy in some way and refuses to pay in full, you can't walk away." I asked him to elaborate. He described a deal that he was negotiating in which the outstanding bill was $40 million. The client didn't want to pay anything, and he had to walk away with $18 million to $20 million or so to "come out okay on the deal." First, I got him to be a bit more precise on his bottom line. Finally, he confessed that the absolute minimum he could accept was $16.8 million. "And if they don't pay that amount?" I asked.

"We will have to sue them, and that would be bad for everybody. We don't want to do that," he said.

"I think I understand, but let me be sure. You expect to settle around the $20 million mark, but they will have to pay at least $16.5 million or else you will have to sue them," I said. He looked at me and slowly realized that indeed he had his Want ($20 million) and his Walk: his "or else" point ($16.5 million). Now all he needed was his Wish and he would be ready to go into battle. He confessed that there were some problems on delivery and that the true amount that should be paid was $34 million.

It was amazing to see this highly experienced negotiator relax into the Wish-Want-Walk method. Obviously, with a deal that size, there was a lot of special and detailed preparation, but he settled the bill at $22 million. He credited his success with the simple framework he had created when he came up with his Wish, Want, and Walk and realized that even in this unpleasant situation he had an option. It was not an option he wanted to exercise, but he had a Walk-Away position.

Your Walk-Away point is not something you want to advertise to the other side. You think about it. You set it. You write it down as part of a short memo to yourself, and you get buy-in from the person to whom you answer. You incorporate it into your Wish, Want, Walk. Then you go into the negotiation armed with this private piece of information. In the majority of situations, the other side will start out well above your Walk-Away point and the negotiation will close in your Want area. In these cases, you will not have to visit your Walk position again. There are always times when the other side takes you close to your Walk-Away position on one or more of the issues that are in negotiation. It happens. But you are prepared because you thought about your Walk Away before you entered the negotiating room. You are ready.

When the negotiation approaches your Walk-Away position, you start giving a lot of signals, both verbal and nonverbal, that you don't have any more room. You also start looking for other elements that you can make more important.

Your Power Is Rooted in Your Walk

Each of us creates doubts about our power in a situation. The ideal mind-set to achieve the best deal is that the world is a plentiful place. There is always somewhere else to sell your wares or satisfy your needs. You don't need to do business with any specific person. Not feeling that you have power comes from a wrong-headed view of the universe. You can always do business somewhere else and with someone else. You are never at the mercy of the one person you happen to be negotiating with at the moment. No matter how much you want something, there is always somewhere else to get it. Do not ever think that you are stuck with only one choice in life.

Often my writer clients think they have no power in a negotiation with a big studio. I always have to convince them that indeed they have the power to sell the script to another studio and that the particular studio we are talking to would not be at the table if it did not want the script. My task is not always easy. The writer has spent solitary months writing the script, and it may have been turned down by two or three other studios before this one showed any interest. I have to convince them that there are always other studios and that there are other ways to get a film made outside the studio system. Once they have those facts firmly in mind, I can negotiate a much better deal for them.

It is the other choices that give you power in a negotiation. Once you know that you have other choices, you decide which one of those choices you will exercise if the negotiation doesn't result in a deal that makes you happy. That is an essential step in establishing your Walk Away. That step gives you real power in a negotiation.

I first met my agent, the incredible Jan Miller, at the Bel-Air Hotel in Los Angeles for breakfast. I was a bit nervous because I had heard so many great things about this super book agent who represents Oprah Winfrey, Dr. Phil, Tony Robbins, my friend Tom Sullivan, Allan Mayer—who had introduced us—and a very few others. As she approached the table, she held out her hand, announced her name, and said, "I loved your Wish-Want-Walk concept. Especially the Walk. People don't know what power there is in knowing that you can Walk Away. I am always ready to Walk if the deal isn't right." Then she regaled me with the story of how she had walked away from a deal she was offered by Microsoft. They had sent a six-member negotiating team, each one impeccably dressed, to her Dallas office to persuade her to let them put some books by her clients on their e-book site and how great it would be for them. She kept telling them that the terms were too one-sided. They didn't budge. She didn't budge. Eventually, she walked away with those valuable publishing rights in hand until she found a fair and balanced deal for her authors. Even in the retelling of the story over a year after it happened, I could sense the pride and energy Jan felt from enforcing her Walk-Away point. Knowing your Walk-Away point before you start a negotiation is a source of genuine power.

Knowledge Is Power

People hear this so often that they sometimes discount the fundamental, far-reaching truth of the statement. If you glance at the first few chapters of this book, you will note that each of the chapters dedicated to forming your Wish, your Want, and your Walk is focused on the knowledge you should have before you start negotiating.

Knowledge is power. The better prepared you are, the more confident you will be during the negotiation. It is knowledge of the subject matter that allows you to speak fluidly, answer questions with alacrity, and overcome objections with clear explanations. Nothing replaces preparation when you sit down to negotiate.

The Power of Numbers

There are certain times when you realize that you can't achieve something you would like to accomplish all by yourself. Laborers in mines, mills, and factories form unions to achieve improvements in wages and working conditions that can't be achieved through individual requests. This applies to many types of negotiations.

For instance, the Discovery Channel recently revised the standard credit language in its producing contract, moving the end-roll credits from the television screen to its website. In the television industry, careers are made and broken on the credits and where they appear. They may be boring to the outsider, but the screen credits are the final authority that the industry uses to determine what one does or does not do on a particular picture or episode. Credits have been called the lifeblood of the industry.

When individual producers called Discovery to complain about the new policy, they were stonewalled. We formed the Documentary Credits and within a few weeks 16 unions, dozens of other organizations, and a lot of high-powered producers had signed on. We had meetings and developed a clear Wish (traditional unlimited credits), Want (some limited on-screen credits), and Walk (no credits). It took a while to get Discovery to listen to us, but ultimately we reached a compromise exactly at our Want.

That never would have happened without the power of numbers. Note that numbers seldom are enough. It took a well-thought-out Wish-Want-Walk plan with Wishes that were limited, a realistic and well-informed Want, and a Walk that turned out to be a rallying cry for a broad spectrum of folks in the industry. Even a large number of people can be crushed if they do not have a solid plan.

The Power of Principle

Even in this highly secular age, there is power in taking a position as a matter of principle. Moral and ethical principles still grab people's attention. In choosing such a position, you must be tactful so that you do not inadvertently paint the people you are trying to persuade as unprincipled or untrustworthy. Both sides to a negotiation can agree that it is important to take an ethical approach to business.

Businesses that focus on their principles tend to thrive. When a frost in Brazil drove up the price of high-quality coffee, many coffee shops and retailers were "forced" to cut the quality of their coffee by mixing less expensive coffee into their blends to keep the price at a level that would not annoy consumers. Starbucks could implement only a small price increase but still refused to lower the quality. They went into the marketplace and made long-term contracts with quality growers around the world. It helped that they already had good relationships with growers. They struggled and even took a hit in their profits, but they came through the crisis with an enthusiastic customer base and with their principles intact. They did that by letting their principles control all their decisions, including negotiations with growers around the world.

Too many people have lost sight of the connection between principled behavior and success in business. Over time and throughout the world, principles prevail. Sometimes it is hard to see this with all the news of corporate misbehavior in the papers. Keep in mind that such behavior makes the newspapers because it is the exception, not the prevailing rule. When in doubt, do the right thing.

The Power of Passion

Another great source of power to those who may feel weak or disadvantaged in some way in a negotiation is the power of passion. There are many stories in show business of people who were sustained and ultimately succeeded against all odds, powered purely by their passion. Sometimes passion is so strong that it communicates more strongly than words can say, "I'm not ever giving up. You have to pay attention to me!" My favorite story about the power of passion came from a Hispanic van driver named Carolyn Mascareñas, who picked me up at the airport for a negotiation seminar.

She knew me from some previous visits, so we started talking on the way to the seminar site. Like most people, she had a fascinating story to tell.

As a conscientious single mom, Carolyn worked hard while helping raise her middle-school son Phillip. One night she happened to pick up one of his books. She was appalled to read a story describing one of the characters, Juanita, as dirty, sloppy, and inattentive. None of the other characters were described by their ethnicity. None of the other characters were described as dirty. And "dirty" had nothing to do with any other aspect of the story. She found other pages in the same book in which kids with negative characteristics had Hispanic names.

She went to the school board and without being on the agenda (and without staying within the time frame) this mother—who had never spoken in public before—pleaded for a change in the text. After many turn-downs and defeats along the way, the state board of education changed the text. A year and a half later, the book was revised so that the offensive stereotypes were removed from the book across the country—all at the publisher's expense. Carolyn never was joined by any of the forces you would expect to speak up on such issues. She carried the negotiation all by herself.

One woman. One voice. Her passion was unstoppable. Passion is its own source of power.

Walking Away in Personal Relationships

I am often asked questions about using the Wish-Want-Walk method in negotiations that involve personal relationships. The people who have asked me those questions have taught me an important lesson: The Wish, Want, Walk method is very helpful in the most difficult of all negotiations: those involving personal relationships.

Oddly, it is the concept of establishing your Walk-Away point ahead of time that often proves to be the most helpful. Every couple caught up in the first flush of love is filled to overflowing with their Wish. That is where couples freshly in love seem to live. They are also aware of their Want. They know somewhere in the back of their minds that there will be laundry and cooking and kids and bills and schedules and all the mundane things that make up everyday life. The Walk-Away point, however, is seldom thought of, let alone mentioned. It might put a hex on the relationship.

However, if you don't think about the Walk Away point ahead of time, if you don't set it out clearly in your mind and, I hope, on paper, you will be like many people in a personal relationship who did not set their limits. They go along and get along until one day one of them shouts to the other, "Now you've done it. You really crossed the line that time!"

Generally, the other party is thinking, "What line? I didn't see any line. What is this all about?" If the offended party had thought out the "line"—the Walk—he or she could have articulated it calmly and early in the relationship during an interesting conversation about what is important in life. Then, if something came up in the relationship that was akin to the Walk-Away position of either party, both people would know it. Both people would be aware that there was the potential for a problem if things kept going in the same direction. In most instances, the fact that both sides are aware of the Walk-Away point keeps the line from being crossed. If there is a compromise that can be worked out, there is time to find it calmly and rationally before unstated boundaries have been violated. If there is no compromise to be worked out, the parties can go their separate ways in peace, knowing that they tried and that there was no solution. Much of the anger after a divorce comes from the fact that unstated boundaries—the Walk position—were crossed and anger set in before the parties realized how much trouble they were in.

To preserve your relationship, you must think about and talk about your Walk-Away point—those things that are unacceptable. Do this well ahead of time instead of hiding it, as you would in a business negotiation. Ideally, a couple discovers during the courtship whether the other person is likely to violate any of the Walk-Away points. The information comes to them intuitively. Sometimes that doesn't happen. More often, people don't consciously think about the Walk-Away point during courtship. In a personal relationship, get the things that make up your Walk-Away position on the table early. Talk about them thoroughly before making the relationship permanent. It will pay off in years of happiness.

Chapter 5

GETTING READY
TO USE YOUR
WISH-WANT-WALK PLAN

WE HAVE INTRODUCED YOU TO THE POWER OF THE WISH, Want, Walk method, including one chapter each on establishing your Wish, understanding your Want, and setting your Walk-Away point. Let's assume that you are heading into a negotiation and have followed the method faithfully up to this point. You have done all your research and decided on a manageable number of Wishes. You understand the marketplace thoroughly and therefore understand your Want. You know your Walk and are prepared to enforce it fearlessly. This chapter is designed to help you make the best use of the time between the creation of your Wish, Want, Walk and the moment when you go into your first negotiating session. This

chapter is like that last look in the mirror to be sure
that your hair is not mussed and there is no spinach
between your teeth.

Be Sure to Have Buy-in

To achieve your dreams and goals, you must build a
field of agreement. There is hardly ever such a thing
as a two-party negotiation. If you and I do a deal, we
each will have someone who has a stake in the outcome, either a business stake or a personal stake. We
each have to bring whoever that person is to a point
of agreement. Once you have agreement with the
stakeholders on your Wish-Want-Walk plan, you
have sown the seeds for success.

Identify the people in your company who need
to be on the same page. Certainly everybody who is
going to be in the room with you during the negotiation has to be on the same page. Your boss and
whoever else has final approval over the deal have to
be on the same page. And then there is that pesky
assistant or secretary or upward-bound middle manager who will put in his or her two cents despite
being nowhere in the chain of command on this particular deal. I strongly recommend that you face that
reality and be sure that person is also on the same
page. It is usually someone who is mildly (or more)
annoying to you because you perceive him or her
to be a busybody, poking his or her nose where it
doesn't belong. Either involve such people infor-
mally before the negotiation or brace yourself for

uninformed commentary on your performance after the negotiation has been completed.

> You can build a field of agreement around any Wish you have. Sometimes that takes some planning. When Bob Uhler became president of the engineering company MWH Global, he wanted to change the way the company negotiated contracts. He wanted the contracts to be based on value instead of the number of labor-hours invested. He knew that the shift had to take place in the minds of hundreds of employees spread out in offices all across the United States. He started by convincing the top rung of executives. Then he and Betsy Redfern launched a training course that taught the principles he believed in. I was pleased to be the facilitator for that course. He once commented to me, "If you want to start a revolution, you first capture the radio station." Within three short years, the negotiators for MWH were all speaking the same language and negotiating contracts on the basis of the value of the engineering services they provided instead of the old-fashioned hour-based fees that had hobbled the company for many years. Bob Uhler built a field of agreement around his concept of changing the way the company negotiated, and then the changes followed.

To build your dream, to achieve your Wish, first build a field of agreement around it. Build a field of agreement around your Walk. Be very sure that everyone agrees on what is not acceptable. And of course, everyone should be in alignment on your Want—what the market usually will bear.

Role Playing

When you have set your Wish, Want, Walk, role playing is one of the most helpful things you can do just before a negotiation commences. Role playing is a realistic interactive rehearsal that will help you during a negotiation. If you have a negotiating team, it is one of the best ways to put the finishing touches on your preparation. It also helps pull the team into a working unit. Everyone on the team has a chance to critique an answer, evaluate a position, or suggest an alternative way to express your position—all in the safety of your own workspace.

Role playing is not memorizing. It is realistically practicing your presentation, complete with interruptions and questions. Talking to a mirror is not realistic and can mislead you into thinking you are ready when you are not.

The role-playing process helps you no matter which side you take in the practice sessions. If your role is that of your future adversary, you will gain as much as or more than you will if your role is the same one you will have in the negotiation. If you play your adversary, you gain insights into the other side's point of view and how he or she is likely to react to the proposals your team will be making. You will understand your adversary's position better. Getting inside the adversary's head is enormously helpful to you and your team.

Not long ago, a gentleman in one of my seminars told me that he had prepared very, very well for a negotiation and yet everything still went wrong. He said that he had never prepared better for anything in his life and it was his most disastrous negotiation ever.

When I pressed for details, he told me how he said everything he had planned to say exactly as he had planned to say it, and the other side became irritated. As he continued, the other side became more irritated.

This was too interesting to let pass. I pressed further. He then described how he had written out exactly what he wanted to say and memorized it and practiced with his wife, who agreed that it perfectly summarized what he should say to close the deal. The problem was obvious to me.

This man replaced preparation with memorization. In fact, he wasn't very well prepared. He had his Wish well in hand but he did not have much knowledge about the subject of the negotiation (the Want) and he knew almost nothing about the person with whom he was negotiating. When he gave his speech, it was not responsive to what the other person had been saying to him. No wonder the other side became irritated. As he continued with his memorized speech, the other side just became more irritated.

When you know the subject matter of the deal inside and out and you know your company's Wish, Want, Walk, the words will flow easily. There is no substitute for knowledge. Careful preparation of your Wish, Want, Walk is what will carry the day. When you really know your stuff, you can rely on your own style and your own words as they fit conversationally into the discussion.

A memorized speech hits the mark no more often than those quick quips they teach in some seminars work on a regular basis. The reason a canned speech or a ready remark doesn't work is that neither one leaves room for listening. Once you have memorized exactly what you are going to say, there is no need to listen, and you probably won't. Know the message you want to get across, listen to your opposite number, and then speak from the heart.

Negotiating as a Corporate Skill

Negotiating is a team sport. As soon as one person tries to be the star, the whole team can be hurt. Sure, there is the occasional razzle-dazzle result and one person gets most of the high-fives. But over time and throughout dozens of situations against a variety of negotiating teams and styles on the other side of the table, it is the best team that wins, not a single star negotiator.

No matter how talented the individuals are as negotiators, they will be even more effective if certain things are true about your company. I call this the company's negotiating culture. The best negotiating teams come from companies with a strong negotiating culture. Here are five hallmarks of a company that produces consistently strong negotiating teams:

1. The company has a strong negotiating infrastructure. Whether you use the Wish-Want-Walk method or another negotiating approach, the entire company should be clued in to what the method is all about, how it works, and why it works. The negotiating training has to be planned to be continuous for several years at all levels, including (maybe especially) the highest executive level of the company.

2. The employees share the negotiating vocabulary. A lot of companies let every executive pick whatever course he or she wants to take on negotiating. There are a lot of good courses out there. The assumption is that they will learn a lot of different tips and some day the various executives will know, among themselves, all there is to know about negotiating. The logic is understandable, but it doesn't work that way in the real world. A better solution is for the company to decide on one approach to negotiating and have everybody on the team use that approach. That way they can pass the ball back and forth with the same vocabulary around negotiating. Each employee sees himself or herself as part of a large negotiating team. Everyone is on the same page. It is the most effective way. Whatever course your company uses, whether it is a course that uses the Wish-Want-Walk method, the Harvard BATNA approach, or the Wharton Business School's "framing" and "throwing your anchor," everyone should have the same vocabulary. At the end of the day, all the negotiating courses are talking about the same thing. There are no deep, dark secrets about negotiating. All good negotiating courses cover about the same ground.

3. The corporate culture has to encourage everyone to use his or her own style within the general infrastructure the company has adopted. There can be no insistence on a single style of negotiating.

4. Negotiators must be evaluated on something other than the final price. For instance, when the

Wish-Want-Walk method is used, the test of a good negotiation is how well the negotiators did compared with what they had listed in each category as their Wish, Want, Walk. It's common to see a salesperson hold out on price because that is how he or she is measured but then give away the store in terms of warranty, service, or assumption of risk.

5. The negotiators must be comfortable walking away from a deal. A Walk in the appropriate situation must be honored and rewarded by the company and coworkers with the same respect as closing a really big deal.

If your company meets all these criteria, you have an excellent chance of building a good negotiating team. If your company does not meet all these criteria, your team is at an inherent disadvantage. They don't have the vocabulary or context to talk to each other about how they plan to go about the negotiation. You might end up with a good result on certain negotiations, but overall, the best negotiating teams come from companies with the best negotiating culture.

Right Before the Negotiation Begins

Face-to-face meetings often occur after a race through traffic, sometimes with a good deal of the drive spent on a cell phone. Even experienced negotiators will run into a room with the stress of traffic written all over their faces. They often blurt out apologies for being late and regale whoever will listen with stories of road repairs, accidents along the way, or whatever it was that held them up.

Before you start any important negotiation, take a small break. Even a break of less than a minute helps. It can be in your car, in the parking lot, or as you put your hand on the door of the negotiating room. Go inside yourself. Pull your focus onto the task at hand: the negotiation.

Before a sporting event begins, you always see the football team or basketball team take a moment of quiet together for a few inspirational words or a prayer. Gymnasts always take a moment before they start a routine. An actor pauses a moment in the wings before going on stage. No matter how skilled they are and how warmed up they are, world-class athletes and world-class performers know the importance of that final moment of quiet and connection. If you want to be a world-class negotiator, you will do the same thing.

As you pull out of your reverie, quickly remind yourself of your Wish, your Want, and your Walk. Then focus on your Wish. Don't worry about how you will express your Wish or when you will present it. Just keep a picture in your mind of your Wish, your goal. Go into the room with that picture in your mind. You will do just fine.

Part II

HOW WISH, WANT, WALK GUIDES YOU IN THE ROOM

Chapter 6

HOW WISH, WANT, WALK TAKES THE FEAR OUT OF MAKING THE OPENING OFFER

▲ ▲ ▲

WHERE TO START? Who starts? When to start?

The questions that surround the opening offer are the negotiator's equivalent of a writer with writer's block, an actor with stage fright, and an orator who is tongue-tied. The fear of screwing things up right from the beginning gives many negotiators cold, clammy hands before they reach out to shake hands. They are afraid they will lose some advantage, "leave money on the table," or "start too low." In fact, it is the apprehensions about making the opening offer that cause much of the fear around negotiation. These feelings are natural if you haven't worked out your Wish, Want, Walk. They are the reason so many people grab on to one of the few (but false) "rules" of negotiating: Never make the first offer. The real rule is that there are no rules, only principles for you to tailor in your own way. You need the confidence to believe in those principles.

Let's look at Wish, Want, Walk to see if it can help you get started. Let's assume you have established your position for your Wish, your Want, and your Walk. You should be ready to start negotiating, but you are unsure of your opening offer. Look at the graphic below. It represents the three positions you have on a particular issue in the negotiation. Take a pencil and place a mark next to the point where you want to make your first offer.

Don't be shy. Put a mark right where you would want to make the first offer.

WISH

WANT

WALK

You are absolutely right. Your first offer should always be at or slightly above your wish. If you start anywhere below your Wish, you have given up a piece of your dream before you get started. There they are—your hopes—dashed on the rocks of timidity before they were articulated.

A Wish that was developed according to the process described in Chapter 2 deserves better treatment than a speedy and silent abandonment. If you brainstormed all the possibilities for your Wish list and then systematically narrowed the list to a manageable number of items, your efforts should be honored. Your Wish list contains only Wishes that are specific, are you-centric, are a stretch, are time-coded, have buy-in from everybody, and are manageable. You carefully created your notion of the true value of the item being negotiated. Now you must put it out to the world. When you tell the person on the other side of the table about your concept of value, there is only a slim chance that the two of you will have a common vision of value. That rarely happens, but at least you have stated your Wish. Then the other side can state its vision of the value—its Wish. The two of you have defined the negotiating field. Know this to be true: Your Wish is the best you're ever going to get. A negotiation will never improve from your Wish. That just doesn't happen.

"Ah," you say, cocking your head back with the wisdom of one who has been there, done that. "It is better to give a little ground at the outset than to scare someone away right at the beginning." My answer is that like so many things in life, it is not what you do but how you do it. The more solid you are with your Wish, the more important it is for you to make the first offer. The distance between your Wish and your Walk will dictate how you "frame" that first offer.

Framing Your Offer

When you think of framing an offer, think of the frame around a picture in a gallery. The frame often costs as much as the picture. If you are framing a poster, the frame almost always costs more than the poster. But we all know that putting the right frame around a poster or print can make it look very special and very valuable. It takes time to look at various frames to select the right one. Then hanging it on the wall in just the right position adds to the impression that the print is important, that it is a thing of value. If you take that amount of time to select the frame for a poster, maybe you should take at least that much time to select the frame for your opening offer.

Unlike some other parts of the actual negotiations, you always have some time to think about your opening offer. Therefore, think about the offer and how you are going to frame it. Think about how to tell your story around the opening offer. What is it that is so attractive about your offer as far as the other party is concerned? Create a metaphor if you can. Make it smell sweet. Make the music soar. Paint a picture. Set the mood.

That may sound a bit over the top, but that is your job in a negotiation. No matter what you call it, your job is to make your opening offer the prettiest girl at the prom. Dress it up any way you need to—without stretching the truth—and then your opening offer will not scare anyone away. It may even attract a few suitors.

When Lee Iacocca was president of Chrysler, the company was in big trouble and felt that the only way out was a bailout by Uncle Sam. Word got out about Iacocca's plan, and the reaction was swift and harsh. Charity to one of the world's largest corporations? Not a good idea. Iacocca didn't ask Congress for a bailout. He asked Congress to pass a jobs preservation act, and it did. Who could argue against such a worthy cause?

That's called framing.

Framing is my word for how you present your arguments. A great frame around a picture or poster makes it look terrific. The wrong frame detracts a lot from the presentation. Let's start with the simplest example, one that requires no imagination. Let's say your Wish is way above your Want; that is, your goal is way above the place where the negotiation is most likely to end up depending on all the market forces at play in the negotiation. You know from Chapter 2 that you are going to put your Wish on the table even though the likelihood of achieving it is slim. Otherwise, you will have abandoned your dream without ever giving it a chance. Thus, the issue becomes how you frame your Wish. You certainly don't present your Wish as a take-it-or-leave-it proposition. You present it as something you would like to achieve in an ideal world, but you realize that it is not to be attained in this negotiation. You say that you are mentioning your Wish because you think the process deserves that sort of candor. If there is very little space between your Wish and your Want (and perhaps equally little between your Want and your Walk), you make that clear: "Here is our opening offer, and I am afraid I have very little room to negotiate on that price."

Once you get the idea of framing down pat, you can take it to the next level by finding metaphors to use when you present an idea. Anne Miller wrote a whole book on how to create metaphors to make ideas attractive. It's called *Metaphorically Selling*. Chief Justice John Roberts dazzled a hostile Senate committee by turning dry legal explanations into baseball metaphors. On the touchy issue of judicial activism, he likened himself (if confirmed) to an umpire simply calling balls and strikes. Many observers think that the metaphors Roberts used went a long way toward ensuring his confirmation by the full Senate. A little accuracy may be sacrificed, but the argument becomes much more palatable and much more persuasive. Roberts continues using metaphors in his written decisions. In finding that an officer was justified in entering a home without a warrant when he observed a serious fight in progress, Roberts wrote, "An officer is not like a boxing referee, poised to stop a bout only if it becomes too one-sided."

Check out the way political proposals are presented to see how a bad idea can be dressed up and presented in a very favorable way. Take a tip from those who are good at sound-bite presentations of an idea even if you are on the other side politically.

A wonderful commercial artist learned about the importance of framing a lesson well. One of her best clients was a well known company, which had had her design five of the many dolls it had produced over the years.

One day an executive from the company called her to say that they were cleaning up their files and noticed that she had not assigned the copyright on the designs to them. They would be sending over "a little piece of paper" for her to sign and would be happy to pay her $35,000 for her trouble.

That was the same amount they had paid her to make the original drawings. It was an amount that would make anybody sit up and take notice. It was an amount that sent her immediately to my colleague Alan Harris. She didn't want to give up her copyright at all. She knew that she could not go out and use these designs for other clients, but she took pride in her work and made it a practice to hold on to the copyrights of everything she designed—unless she was paid absolutely full value for them.

Her Walk was clear: hang on to the $35,000. Don't scare them away. None of us knew exactly why the company had called so unexpectedly, but we figured the Want had to be between $50,000 and $100,000. What about the Wish? It took some cajoling, but finally she said, "If I have to give up my copyright, I want a million dollars." By presenting the Wish as just a Wish and not a take-it-or-leave-it demand, Alan didn't scare the company away. He stated the Wish clearly and firmly and explained her practice of holding the copyright as a matter of professional pride. He was framing the issue carefully. Eventually they paid $750,000 for the rights they sought.

A Wish not stated is a Wish denied. But framing is important. Often people are reluctant to express a Wish for fear of driving away the other side. It is important always to state your Wish. How you frame your Wish is absolutely critical.

Is this our first rule of negotiating? Should we always put the Wish on the table first? Your first move always depends on the circumstances. If your Wish is strongly at odds with your Want, you need to be sure that you can present your Wish face to face with enough time to frame it; if you can't do that, don't present your Wish at all. If circumstances don't allow you to frame a Wish that is seriously at odds with your assessment of Want, you might think about presenting something closer to reality. For instance, if you are buying a house, the chances are that you are going to present an offer in writing through your realtor to the seller's realtor. Your offer goes through the hands of two busy people before it reaches the only person you need to persuade: the seller of the house. Any explanation you give will be distorted or dropped entirely in the process of passing your offer through two agents to the seller. This is why your opening offer should be very close to your Want when you are negotiating a home purchase. There is no chance to explain your offer adequately to the seller—you don't get to frame your offer.

It contains no explanation of how much you love the property and no assurances about your plans to preserve the look and feel of the property. It just lies there, unframed and unattractive. You have to be careful about where you place your Wish if you aren't able to frame it properly.

Who Makes
the First Offer?

Once you know exactly how much to offer or demand and have an idea about how to frame it, turn your attention to whoever makes the first offer. Many people believe that you should always let the other guy make the first offer. They think that is one of the primary rules of negotiating.

Letting your counterpart make the first offer is not so much a rule as it is an excuse. It turns the fear of making the first offer into something that sounds much more acceptable. This "rule" has allowed many negotiators to avoid thinking through the first offer. They feel that they don't have to figure out their Wish or how to present it. What would the world be like if everybody insisted on letting the other person make the first offer? In fact, the best negotiators focus on the advantages of taking a certain course of action rather than allowing their fears or rules to dictate the negotiation.

The rule—if there is such a thing—is that it depends. If you don't know what you are doing, if you haven't done your homework, *never* make the first offer. However, if you do know what you're doing, there are certain advantages in setting the tone of the negotiation by throwing out the first number.

When you make the first offer, the other side often will alter its position as soon as it hears your offer. They will say to themselves, "Gee, if we want this deal, we will have to spend more than we planned." Psychological studies confirm that when the other side throws out a number that is higher or lower than expected, the human tendency is to move one's opening position closer to that of the other side without mentioning one's preset Wish.

At the Wharton School of Economics, this is called anchoring the negotiation. There are sometimes real and clear benefits to making the first offer. In my business, the best example of the need to make the first offer is when a producer wants a free option to purchase a project. Obviously, there is nothing cheaper, and so you want to beat the other person to the punch.

You want to "anchor" the negotiation by mentioning the free option first. It is a dead certainty that the other side is never going to start the discussion by offering a "free option."

Developing a solid position for your Wish is the key to being able to make the first offer without fear. With a solid Wish position, you will know exactly where to make the first offer. Most of the stories I read and hear that illustrate the wisdom of the rule "always make sure the other person goes first" are better illustrations of the need for a solid Wish-Want-Walk plan. Almost always the stories end with a "wow, isn't it good we didn't put out our foolish low number before we knew what they would be willing to offer." My silent reaction is, "Wow, how could you have thought that your foolish low number was the correct first offer? What made you think you were ready to make the first offer? It was a foolish low offer, and you should have known it. You hadn't done your homework!"

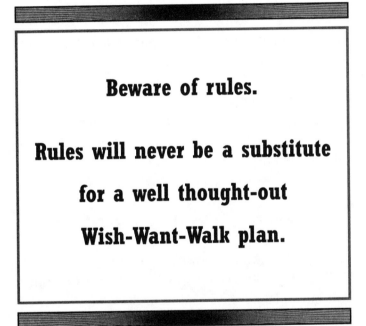

Beware of rules.

Rules will never be a substitute
for a well thought-out
Wish-Want-Walk plan.

If the other side makes the first offer, do not modify your Wish. Be sure to mention it even if the offer by the other side makes it clear that you are never going to obtain it. By stating your Wish you are defining the range of possible places for the negotiation to settle. You are setting the playing field. Make it as large as reasonably possible.

Often the person making the offer second will mention something less than their Wish even though they never would have done that after making the first offer. That is a big mistake.

Several university studies show that such unnecessary, unrecompensed concessions occur with alarming frequency. This silent retreat can cost you dearly because you have given up ground that the other side did not even know existed.

When to Make the First Offer

Let's assume you are confident in your Wish, Want, Walk and you know you should make the first offer. You have picked the location and are sitting across from your opposite number. You are ready to make an offer. Don't let that be the first thing you do at the start of the negotiation session. Always take time to establish rapport and do some additional preparation by probing the other side to determine its interests and its needs and wants.

Sometimes it depends on the time of day. As I was writing this chapter, I was in the middle of negotiating insurance coverage for a film that was about to go into theatrical release. The conversations had

The answer to almost every question about good negotiating:

It depends.

been rushed because time was slipping away and the distributor was threatening to cancel the release. My final conversation with the underwriter at the insurance company was on a Friday afternoon. It was the last call of the day for both of us. We relaxed into the conversation and talked about our weekend, our sisters, and how we were taking up the slack for a lot of other people who had put off this issue for far too long. We eased into the negotiation and ended up closing the deal that afternoon with a solution that made our clients and us very happy. Our slower pace actually sped up the closing of the deal.

How much time you spend on introductory matters depends on the personalities and cultures of the people involved in the negotiation. In Japan, there will be meetings and dinners galore before the first offer is made. In fact, there will be meetings and dinners before the Japanese are sure that they want to make an offer to do business with you at all. This introductory time and the opinions that are formed are often as important as the deal itself. This is even more true in China, where the contract is little more than an agreement to do business together in the future, solve problems as they come up, and go forward in good faith. Because of this attitude, it is imperative that the parties be comfortable with each other before they start negotiating.

People raised in the culture of Middle Eastern nations often use the introductory time to present offers and counteroffers that are not intended to be accepted. Rather, they are designed to get to know you and how you react to various situations. The potential jousting helps them decide whether to invite you into their business family. Doing business in this part of the world is a much more familial activity than is doing business in the Western world generally and the United States in particular.

Once again, the answer to the question of when to make the first offer is: It depends. It depends on many cultural elements, some of which I mentioned above. It depends on how well you know the person. It depends on how many preliminary conversations you have had. It depends on what you already know about what the other side needs and wants. It depends on your personality.

There are a lot of resources to use if you don't trust your gut on the issue of how fast to move. No matter what culture or country you visit, there are books to read. There are also a number of personality tests you can take to see how you measure up against the general population regarding your desire to move things along. Two notable sources are the widely used Meyers-Briggs Type Indicator Test and the hugely effective tests that measure your instincts designed by Kathy Kolbe. You will know if you are the type to rush things along and lack sensitivity to other people's needs or if you are the plodding type who doesn't like to be rushed into making a decision. Most people are not surprised by the test results. The tests help compare your issues of timing with those of other people you may encounter. They help you understand that neither party is wrong. There are simply different ways of being in the world.

Some people by nature are in a hurry and want to get down to business quickly. Other people like a slower pace and want to spend a lot of time in the preliminary stage of getting to know you. Within every culture, people come in a wide variety of personality types. Don't stereotype people by their cultural background in this modern multicultural world.

Your Place or Mine?

Another common "rule" of negotiating is that you should always negotiate on your home turf. Once you have established your Wish-Want-Walk plan, it won't make much difference where you negotiate. Sure, your place is more comfortable. You have more control over the seating and other aspects of the environment. If there is a power seat in the room, you can capture it before the other side arrives. There are a lot of advantages to negotiating on your home turf.

However, if you hold meetings at the offices of your counterpart, you will have other advantages. A number of excuses for delay by the other side will evaporate, such as not having certain facts or figures or needing a quick conversation with somebody. Those excuses carry a lot less weight when you are in their office, where their files are handy and that person is right down the hall. If the other person has to consult with someone or obtain some approvals, it will be easier to have that happen if you are already in that person's office. All the physical aspects of the meeting will be easier for the other person. That will make him or her more comfortable and therefore more likely to open up to you.

When you are in someone else's office, you can observe what is important in the other person's life from the details you see in his or her office, such as family pictures. You can observe that person's taste in art. You can learn a lot from travel pictures. A quick eye scan of the office tells you more information than does an hour of conversation. You can usually tell something about where the person fits in the pecking order of the organization. Notice how far the office is from the boss's office. Notice the size of the office compared to other offices.

Always consider the Walk aspect as well. It is easy to walk away from someone else's office. It can be tricky to throw a person out of yours if you want to cut off the discussion and he or she refuses to leave.

As with other questions about negotiating, the answer to the question of where to negotiate is "It depends." Don't be shy about going to the other person's office. It shows self-confidence and you just might learn something useful.

Chapter 7

HOW WISH, WANT, WALK HELPS YOU BARGAIN WITHOUT FEAR

THE NICEST THING ABOUT THE Wish-Want-Walk method is that you already know where you are starting (your Wish), what is acceptable (your Want), and what will not work (your Walk). As the negotiation moves from your Wish position to your Walk position, the concessions become smaller and tougher to make and are accompanied by more nail biting and gnashing of teeth. This is almost automatic when you have laid out your Wish-Want-Walk beforehand.

Think of your Wish-Want-Walk positions as internal traffic signals wired into your brain for any particular negotiation. Your Walk-Away point is a like a red stoplight in your head. As you get close to the red light, the yellow light starts flashing. You don't even have to think about it. If you erect the red light, the yellow light comes with it. This is the way our minds work. Your Wish is the steady green light that tells you that you are free to move forward without a lot of caution. You have plenty of room to maneuver.

This phenomenon is widely recognized. However, people often think of the dwindling concession phenomenon as a function of time: The longer you negotiate, the smaller the concessions should be. Although that is the way it looks most of the time, the real reason concessions are slower, thinner, and harder to come by as the negotiation progresses is that the parties are moving away from their Wish positions and getting closer to their Walk-Away positions.

Always give some thought before making a concession on any point. That is how you give value to any concession you make. If the other side puts something on the table and you immediately say "Sure" or "Of course," the other side will tighten up inside. They will think they could have gotten a lot more, that they acted too quickly, that they goofed. You never want the other side to feel that way. Each point they win should be of value. You are the one who gives it value. You put value on your concessions by taking time and thinking about them, by pondering alternatives before yielding the point. Your thoughtful pause before making the concession adds real value.

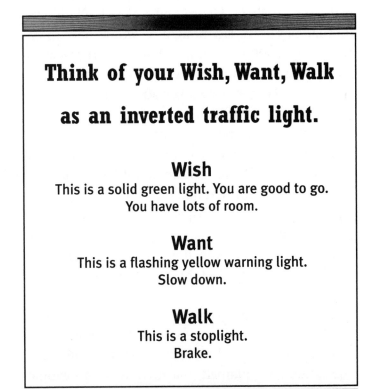

Think of your Wish, Want, Walk as an inverted traffic light.

Wish
This is a solid green light. You are good to go.
You have lots of room.

Want
This is a flashing yellow warning light.
Slow down.

Walk
This is a stoplight.
Brake.

Eddie Gleason of Vernonia, Oregon, learned the psychology of concessions in a way he will never forget. He wanted to buy a tractor for his six-acre property. His wife had just attended a Wish-Want-Walk seminar, and so he used the method as he set out to make the purchase. He wanted a New Holland tractor made by Ford. He thought he would have to pay around $16,000 if he shopped around. That was his Want. He set his Walk at $17,000 and made a Wish at $14,000. He and Amy joked about his ridiculously low Wish as he left the house.

On the way home that night, he stopped at Metro New Holland, a tractor emporium that had many lines of tractors. The salesman told him about a lease-return tractor that had only a few hours of use, had been completely inspected and approved, and would have a full warranty as though it never had been off the showroom floor. The salesman could sell it to him for $14,000, and that included free delivery.

Eddie knew that was a very good deal. He offered $13,500. It wasn't a brand-new tractor, but it was virtually brand-new and he could have it for his Wish! The salesman explained that there was no negotiating because it was a lease-return tractor. Eddie left to think about it but went back the next day, fearing that it would be sold to someone else. He said he also would take the $1,100 mower if they would knock just $200 off the package. Again, the salesman said that the price was fixed on mowers.

Eddie closed the deal but still felt bad about it two months later when he told me the story. He confessed that he happily would have paid $1,000 more if they had started at $2,000 more and then knocked $1,000 off the price.

Eddie told me that he felt strange about his reaction to their failure to negotiate with him because he knew what a great deal he got. After all, he bought the tractor for his Wish number. His feelings are normal. When someone expects to negotiate, always build room for that into your asking price. Eddie and most other people in the world don't like take-it-or-leave-it pricing in situations in which they expect to negotiate.

Eddie is in a home improvement business called Homes New and Old with his old friend Aaron Light. They build new kitchens, new bathrooms, and additions to homes in their area. They used to work out a price and not change it unless something was removed from the scope of the work to be done. They now know to build a little bit into their initial quote that they can give up to make the customer appreciate that he or she is getting a really good price for the high-quality work Eddie and Aaron deliver.

They also build in a little extra for the "unexpected" because "there is always the unexpected." He never charges an additional price just because "we didn't know about it." He thinks it is their job to know. Between their high-quality on-time services and their careful negotiating up front, their business is growing at a very steady pace. They learned the same lesson that Bob Uhler explains in the Foreword: You will never make more profit than you negotiate in the original contract. Once the job starts, the "unexpected" always seems to erode profits, not add to them.

Concessions and Trade-Offs

Most negotiations involve several important categories of bargaining. You need to set down your
Wish, Want, Walk for each category. Let's look at a
case study of a salary negotiation to see how you
arrive at the best solution by creating your own
Wish-Want-Walk plan. A good friend took me out to
lunch to pick my brain about his upcoming salary
negotiation (that's what good friends do; they brain
pick over lunch). I gave my friend a list of categories
and asked him to set up a Wish, Want, Walk for each
category. As he created the Wish, Want, Walk for
each category, he constructed the chart shown in
Figure 7-1. He was very happy and ready to go into
the negotiation.

	Annual Salary	Expenses	Parking	Title	Retirement Plan	Health Plan
WISH	$150,000	All reasonable expenses	Yes	Sr. VP	401K	Full Coverage
WANT	$100,000–$125,000	Up to $500/month w/ receipts	No	VP	401K; profit sharing	Full Coverage
WALK	$90,000	Up to $250/month w/ receipts	No	Director	No pension plan	HMO only option

Figure 7-1

"No, no," I cautioned him. "You are not quite
ready. You need to arrange the columns so that they
are in some order of priority. It will be easier to keep
things straight in your head." He then rearranged
the choices with the most important category on

the left and the least important category on the right. It turned out that he had a child with a chronic illness and so the health plan was enormously important to him. In fact, coverage for that situation was so important that it moved all the way up to a strong second position behind salary, and he added the word *family* so that when he discussed this point with his future employer, he would remember that his definition of "full coverage" would have to be understood to include the entire family (see Figure 7-2).

	Annual Salary	Health Insurance	Retirement Plan	Expenses	Title	Parking
WISH	$150,000	Full Family Coverage	401K expenses	All reasonable	Sr. VP	Yes
WANT	$100,000–$125,000	Full Family Coverage	401K; profit sharing	Up to $500/month w/ receipts	VP	No
WALK	$90,000	HMO only option Full Family	No pension plan	Up to $250/month w/ receipts	Director	No

Figure 7-2

Now he was really happy. He thanked me profusely and ordered the check at the restaurant where we had eaten a fine lunch. "Not so fast," I cautioned. There was one more step. He had developed his Wish, Want, Walk according to categories that I had given him. "Yes," he said "and I really appreciate all your help." He beamed his big, infectious grin. "That's why I'm buying lunch." Gee, thanks, I thought, but what I told him was, "Wait a minute. What is important to me may not be important to you and vice versa." Then I added the obvious: "Look over the list. See if there is a category that I have overlooked or left out."

Sure enough, he realized that he would love an assistant even if he had to share that person with someone else, and as long as he was asking, he might as well ask for an office with a door. He was moving up and his deals were bigger, and he didn't like discussing them with other people listening. He also thought the background noise of an office sometimes made him sound less important than he wanted to sound when discussing a big-ticket item. He added both categories to his list.

Armed with his Wish, Want, Walk for all the categories that concerned him, he was ready to proceed, and proceed he did. He reported that he had never had an initial interview like the one he had for this job. He thought his approach made him more desirable to the company as he came across as an executive-level person instead of someone anxious to get a job—any job—under any conditions. He was ecstatic with the results and found himself enjoying more job satisfaction after he was hired because he had an assistant and an office with a door that closed. The time you spend establishing your Wish, Want, Walk is the most valuable time you spend in any negotiation.

You can picture the whole Wish-Want-Walk method as a glass with a refreshing drink in it. When you are presented with a tall glass of your favorite drink, you are likely to take a large gulp. Then your next sips are normal-size swallows. Near the bottom of the glass you tend to drink slowly; your sips are smaller. That is exactly how a negotiation progresses from Wish, to Want, and occasionally to Walk. Without thinking about the pacing, you are more willing to make large concessions at the beginning, then you slow down as you move to the Want, and when you are near your Walk, the concessions are smaller. You change your position more slowly (Figure 7-3).

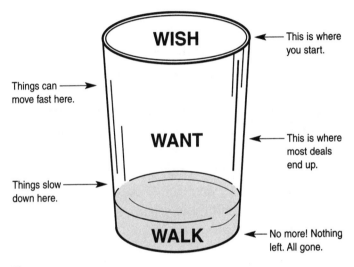

Things can move fast here.

This is where you start.

This is where most deals end up.

Things slow down here.

No more! Nothing left. All gone.

Figure 7-3

Expanding the Pie

One thing you should try hard not to do is let a negotiation get down to one remaining dimension—especially price. When this happens, the negotiation becomes a haggle. Keep multiple items open as the end approaches. Keep your Want firmly in mind so that you will know what concession you can make to close.

We have all been to a used car lot. The first thing the salesperson does is make sure the car you are talking about is the exact car you want. They verify the year, the model, the color, and the mileage, and then they go to work on the price. This is why everyone dreads the negotiation over the purchase of a used car. You want to buy a particular car. The discussion is all about money, and you're not sure what it's worth or if they want much more than it's worth or. . . . Some of those fears can be wiped away with good preparation. You should know a lot about the price of the kind of car you are planning to buy. All that preparation makes you know exactly what your Walk-Away number is, but here you are on the used car lot and have found the perfect car, and suddenly no other car will do.

Let's say the used car salesperson won't budge on the price. In the theater that is the showroom floor, he or she has exited twice to talk to the "manager." "There just isn't any more room," the salesperson says.

I'm still not happy, you say to yourself. You are sure the price is still a tad high, although not past your Walk. You are equally sure the salesperson won't budge, and you want to close the deal. The concessions you could ask for are limited only by your imagination. This is called expanding the pie. Add other elements to what looks like a single-issue negotiation. You may have to push the pause button and take a walk to gather your thoughts. You may use the time while the salesperson is out of the room to consult with the "manager" to come up with some great ideas for expanding the pie.

Here are a few items that have been obtained, some good, some not so good. Some may not be remotely attainable in your situation. I list them here only so that you firmly grasp the idea of expanding the pie. These are just a few ideas from the wide range of things you might ask for:

- Free maintenance for a year

- A free loaner whenever the car is being serviced in the next year

- Free gas for a year

- Free washes and waxes for a year

- A total guarantee on all moving parts for six months

- Free tires after so many miles

Oddly, when you come up with one of these unusual requests, it often is granted. The salesperson initially will say, "Oh, we can't do that." Or, better yet, "We've never done that before." Or maybe even, "My manager will kill me if I ask him that." Persist. Be good-natured about it but persist. Such seemingly off-the-wall requests are granted far more often than you would think. Make sure they understand that if they make this crazy concession that in some cases will not cost them much, you will close the deal at the price they are asking.

Think about your next negotiation. Take a moment and go over a similar list of ideas that will expand the pie if you get stuck on a single issue. Let your imagination fly. There is no limit to the ideas you can come up with. Try it. It's fun to dream up all sorts of things—big and small—that normally would not be on your list. If you give this some thought in advance, you will not freeze up in a tight position. You will be able to come up with various things to use to expand the pie and break the logjam.

Linkage

Linkage is an important concept in negotiating. In the case of the imaginary car purchase we just discussed, linkage will make you feel better about the outcome when the price does not make you all that happy. You have expanded the pie and linked the new element to closing the deal at their price.

Linkage simply means that you agree to some demand from the other side provided that they agree on something that is important to you. There is always something you can link up. If there isn't something that is or has been on the table, you can dream up something else to put on the table. That is called expanding the pie. We talked about this in the preceding section. When you expand the pie, you increase the opportunities for linkage.

Let's suppose you are applying for a new job. Maybe the offer on salary is just under your Want, and they won't budge. The health plan is adequate, but you know that the executives at the next level above you have a much better plan with no preexisting conditions and no deductible. You could link your acceptance of the salary to being placed in the more favorable category for health insurance. That is a classic example of linkage. It is classic because the combination makes you happy even though the salary alone would not make you happy.

Linkage helps close lots of deals. The more complicated the negotiation is, the more opportunities there are to use linkage. When there are a lot of issues, it is only natural to see the connection between some of them. It is also okay to link up unlike items if that will help close the deal.

For instance, you may have exhausted everything on your list. You may link things together until there is nothing left on the list to link. The job could be yours if you would just say yes, but you are still not happy with the salary. Link your acceptance to something that may seem a bit unrelated. For instance, you might want to be introduced around at a certain church in town, or maybe your spouse or partner needs to be hooked up with a group that plays his or her favorite sport. Maybe you want help getting your child into a particular school. I have seen many deals close because linkage was used with wildly disparate elements.

Chapter 8

HOW WISH, WANT, WALK HELPS YOU LEARN TO LISTEN

▲▲▲

I WAS PLEASANTLY SURPRISED as seminar participants started reporting from the field that they were more relaxed when they went into the negotiating room with a clear Wish, Want, Walk. The law of unintended consequences was at work again. That's where a course of conduct is set in motion and the result—or some aspect of the result—is quite different from what you projected. Those participants reported that they didn't worry about making a bad deal or looking bad because the deal didn't close. They knew that they wouldn't get in trouble back home because everyone had agreed on the Wish-Want-Walk plan. They found that they were better able to listen to the other party without interrupting or feeling a need to push their position hard. They were able to listen to the other party, and it is amazing what you learn when you really listen.

You are not going anywhere as a negotiator if you are not a good listener. The best information usually comes from the person with whom you are negotiating. Listen to what that person is saying. This chapter will focus on this important piece of the negotiating puzzle.

Of all the skills that you master, all the tricks that you learn, all the stories that you collect, there is nothing more important in a negotiation than old-fashioned listening. Down through the ages and across all the oceans and lands of the earth, being a good listener is the bedrock of world-class negotiating. Everybody who teaches negotiating and everybody who writes on the subject and everybody who has thought about it at all agree on the importance of effective listening.

Americans are notoriously bad listeners. In fact, Americans are the worst listeners in the world according to my observations and almost everyone else's. It's just not what we do well.

The Chinese are stumped by our babbling. The Arabs think it is barbaric. All around the world, there is puzzlement at the way Americans "don't so much listen as they wait for their turn to talk," to quote the English satirist Evelyn Waugh.

Scientists who study this sort of thing say that Americans are hardwired to be in a rush. It has to do with our relationship to time. Americans view time as precious and finite and feel that life has a beginning and an end and that we have to get everything done quickly—in this lifetime. We are in such a hurry to pile up whatever good deeds we are going to pile up in this lifetime that we don't take time to stop and smell the roses, let alone listen to others. Even our loved ones occasionally are shortchanged when it comes to the time we are willing to spend in the simple act of listening.

The predominant belief system in many parts of the world says that we come back to this earth again and again. In those cultures, people are not in such a hurry to get everything accomplished in this lifetime. They view their time on earth very differently. They are far more inclined to listen to their fellow humans. In fact, they are somewhat distrustful of someone who wants to rush to conclude a deal rather than spend a lot of time getting to know each other. So it is that Asians almost always spend a lot more time than Americans and Europeans in talking with and getting to know a potential business associate before shaking hands on an agreement. This can be a source of great frustration to a hurried and harried American. The resistance by Westerners to these preliminaries can be a source of suspicion to Asians.

I am convinced that listening is the toughest skill to teach and to learn. I think the reason for this is that most teachers approach the subject of listening from a superficial, technique-driven perspective. Even in this book, we are about to go over some listening techniques that will be helpful as you work on your listening skills. The real secret to effective listening is much simpler than any of the techniques set forth in the next few pages.

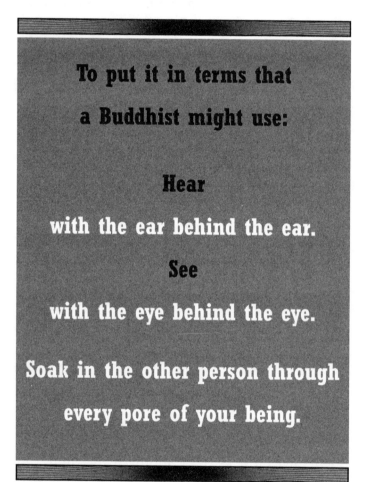

To put it in terms that
a Buddhist might use:

Hear

with the ear behind the ear.

See

with the eye behind the eye.

Soak in the other person through
every pore of your being.

You have to want to listen.

Alan Alda once told me that if you *really* want to listen, you have to be willing to take the risk of being influenced by what the other person says. It took a while for that to sink in, but I think he was on to something. If you open yourself up to being influenced by another person's words and views, you will be much more likely to listen to what that person has to say. True listening always involves the "risk" that you will hear something useful or hear something that changes your mind or learn an unwelcome truth. There is a risk to actively listening to someone else, but the rewards are well worth it.

Active listening is when you listen with a purpose, and that is exactly what you should do in a negotiation. You record the facts, absorb the meaning, and perceive the intentions and feelings behind the words. Listening is not a passive activity during a negotiation. It is work—hard work. If you get tired from all that active listening, take a break, but don't slack off on the listening. It is simply too important.

The world was pleasantly stunned in 1978 when President Jimmy Carter was able to broker an agreement between Egypt and Israel on the Sinai Peninsula. Israel had grabbed that prime piece of real estate in a war, and Egypt wanted it back. There was sand as far as the eye could see. Not a Starbucks in sight. Neither side would back down. The international community was trying to persuade Israel and Egypt to draw a line right down the middle. Neither side was having any of it. A flat refusal from both camps.

President Carter invited the leaders to Camp David. He was fully prepared; he knew both leaders and had had some experience with Middle Eastern affairs. They were equally prepared. All three parties knew the real estate and the issues and the history all too well. They each knew a lot about themselves and the nations they were leading. They each knew a lot about the other parties. Carter held separate sessions with each leader and listened and asked questions.

By stripping away all the rhetoric, he learned that what Israel really wanted was security and what Egypt really wanted was sovereignty. So sovereignty over the Sinai was returned to Egypt, and Israel was allowed to retain its military bases and a demilitarized zone was established as a buffer between Egypt and Israel with the backing of the United States. The two principal nations did not arrive at Camp David with a clear Wish-Want-Walk list. President Carter had to set one up for them by listening to both sides very carefully.

That impossible-to-achieve compromise has lasted to this day. Thirty years later the Sinai Peninsula is still a sea of sand, but that hard-fought turf has not heard a shot fired in anger since the Camp David accords.

**The best tools
for being a
good listener are**

1. Asking questions

2. Paraphrasing back

Asking Questions

When you are really listening to someone speak, you will pick up all sorts of helpful information. You will absorb what the person says and be able to note what has been left out. There are a lot of reasons that information you want is missing from the presentation. The other person may assume you know it. The other person may not want you to know it right away. Most often, the other person is just talking in a normal conversational manner that tends to move away from the detailed and toward the general. That is the way most people talk.

It is your job to get all the information you need.

The best way to do this is by asking questions. Questions are like a child's digging tools. You never know what they will turn up. But if you use them as children use their digging tools, with pure curiosity and absolute interest in whatever you discover, you will turn up true gems. You will find a solution to problems that have puzzled both sides. You will find breakthroughs where none seemed possible. The question that comes from a place of honest interest is one of the negotiator's best friends.

One of my favorite questions is not a question at all. Stated with real curiosity and eye contact, it is a strong declaration of genuine interest. It is an invitation to disclose, to reveal, to be heard. Here it is: Tell me about that.

Over the years, it has opened people up like no other single question I know. I have thought about writing a book about the power of that simple declarative statement that substitutes for a question.

I have another favorite question that I use in really tough spots. It is particularly useful when the position of the other party is totally unacceptable. They have thrown out an idea that simply won't work. Here it is: How would that work?

When they begin explaining how the unacceptable proposal would work, one of three things happens. Sometimes—not often—they will interrupt their own answer with something like, "No, that won't work so well." Sometimes—not often—I will say something like, "Oh, I see, that makes more sense now." Most often, we have a better understanding of what is being proposed and can work together toward a compromise that will work for both sides. But the first step is to ask the probing questions, to find out what exactly the other person is driving at.

Paraphrasing Back

Paraphrasing is a powerful tool to ensure that communications are clear on both sides. It is the simple tool of repeating back to someone what you think that person said. "Let me make sure that I understand that" is a typical introduction to a paraphrasing. "In other words" is another common way to get started. Paraphrase every time you hear anything that is complicated or new to you. Paraphrasing allows you to be absolutely sure that you understand what is being said. It is also a wonderful way of honoring what the other person is saying.

When I reviewed this section of the manuscript, I was concerned that this brief description of paraphrasing might not adequately convey the importance of the technique. Don't judge the technique by the amount of space devoted to it in this book. It is one of the most helpful things you can do to ensure that you heard the other party correctly. Americans find paraphrasing particularly easy to use because it allows you to talk as part of the process of improving the listening.

God gave you four listening devices versus one speaking device for a reason. It is much more important to listen in a negotiation than it is to speak. What you hear will go further toward closing a good deal than almost anything that will come out of your mouth. In fact, your mouth can block the ability of your eyes and ears to do their thing. Your mouth can get you in trouble. It also can be your biggest friend, especially when it stays closed!

Write It Down

This is the strongest technique to make sure you can recall specific data. That is why students who take good notes are almost always the ones who make good grades. The correlation is very high. Be sure someone writes down all the details of any proposal that is presented to you. You want to have the official position of the other side correctly noted.

The more complicated or protracted the negotiation is, the more important it is to have a specific person designated on the team to take notes. Be sure that person knows how important this job is. Ideally, the person selected for the job will not be the lowliest person on the team. That sends the wrong message to everyone about the importance of the task and sometimes causes the wrong message to be recorded. A lack of experience can cause the person to hear something incorrectly.

Be aware, however, that the person who is writing everything down diligently is probably not able to pick up on the subtleties of the message. Less than half the information comes through words. The rest is body language, tone, speed, facial expression, and energy. Somebody needs to be paying attention to that also, especially the lead negotiator.

I worry about what I don't know that I don't know.

The best way to find out what you
don't know is to ask questions
and listen carefully to the answers.
You learn the most surprising
things that way.

My friend and most frequent partner in facilitating my three-day intensive course is Jim Kuiken. He is a great teacher, a loving husband, and a model mentor to his two sons, Andrew and James. His sons wanted a new truck because the old one was not very impressive on dates. Jim put a firm limit on what he would add to whatever they got when they sold the old truck, so they had to make a really good deal and they knew it.

They researched the local papers, searched online, and talked to some car dealers who had the same kind of truck for sale from time to time. Then they listed the truck in the classified ad section of the local paper. After a bit, a potential buyer came by and took it for a test drive. The boys asked a lot of questions and found out that the guy was into four-wheeling. That was all they needed to know. The boys spent the rest of the time talking about the extra-strong four-wheel-drive system and the special low-gear transmission and how the truck could handle rugged off-road driving as well as deep snow: "Remember when we did this?" and "Remember that trip to . . . ?" The stories were great. The laughs were genuine. This curious visitor was genuinely engaged. He wanted to buy the truck. Unfortunately, his first offer was too low, but he left knowing that no matter what else he saw, this particular truck was the one that could take him exactly where he wanted to go. A few days later he came back and met their price.

At first blush, this looks like a great story about setting your Wish, Want, and Walk-Away numbers for selling something and sticking to them, and it is. But the real secret to this sale was asking some probing questions to find out what the other person really wanted. Those two boys learned listening from their dad and got top dollar for their truck in the process, and the buyer drove off with a big smile on his face. In his mind, he was already enjoying his first off-road adventure in his new truck.

I wanted to include this story in the section about asking questions and effective listening because teenagers often are accused of not listening. Too often it is the adults who are not listening to their teenagers. This buyer talked to a lot of other adults during the time between his first visit and his return to buy the truck. He heard about mileage, passenger comfort, and maintenance and reliability. But those two teenage boys were the ones who heard clearly what his real interests were. Let's see how the boys did when they went to purchase a replacement truck.

Andrew and James had to find a truck that fit all their old needs for fun and looked good enough to use on a date. They had the money from the sale of their old truck plus $1,000 from their dad, and they knew they wouldn't get any more from him because Jim is really good at enforcing his Walk Away and they knew it. They did some research, concluded that they wanted a particular model, and kept an eye on the classified ads and dealer lots until they found one. The truck they found was owned by a man who lived in the foothills about an hour's drive outside of town. The boys drove out one Saturday. One of the first things Andrew asked the seller was how much response he was getting to his ad. It turned out that no one had been there in weeks. Andrew talked with the owner and told him that he needed his dad's approval to make an offer, so what was the lowest price he could accept? Andrew called Jim with the number, excited because it was the exact model he wanted and was in great shape. It was over Jim's $1,000 limit, so Jim said "no." He explained that Toyota had made thousands of that model of truck that year. The boys didn't need to buy this particular one. Andrew told the seller that his dad wouldn't put in any more money, so his last offer was the maximum price he could pay. They quickly reached a deal. Andrew was empowered by not having all the power.

This is a great story for many reasons. Jim has a great sense of abundance: You don't have to take every deal because there is always another deal around the corner. It also shows the power of asking questions. Once it was out in the open that the seller wasn't getting nibbles (or even people out to see if they were interested in nibbling at the truck), the possibility of closing at a price Andrew could afford went way up.

The Most Advanced

Communication Technology

of This High-Tech Era

Two chairs

Two people

A lot of time

Chapter 9

HOW WISH, WANT, WALK HELPS YOU NEGOTIATE WITH A JERK

JERKS POP UP RANDOMLY in your life like mushrooms after a spring rain. Sometimes they can make you ill. They are best defined by how you react to them. The reaction usually goes something like this:

ARGGGGGGGGGGGGGGHHHH!!!!!!!!!!!!!!!!!!

You hate sitting across the table from a jerk. It isn't any better when you are sitting on the same side of the table, and sometimes it can be worse. Here is a list of the folks who most often pop up when the discussion in our seminars turns to this subject:

- The liar

- The bully

- The screamer

- The person who loves to put you down

- The person who won't shut up and let
  you talk

- The person who shuts up and lets you talk
  but doesn't listen to anything you say

People also can earn the jerk label by using a terrible tactic no matter how pleasantly they behave. You know the situation: You are cruising along. Everything is going fine. You are somewhere in your Want zone. You figure the deal can close at any time, and suddenly, out of the blue, the other side does something unsuspected, something you are not ready for, something that throws you. There are a dozen dirty tricks that fall into this category. Here are the most common ones:

- Changing an important point at the end of the
  negotiation when you think you have agreed
  on everything

- Agreeing but suddenly needing to check with
  a previously undisclosed partner or boss

- Taking a take-it-or-leave-it stand

- Nickel-and-diming you to death

- Playing a last-minute game of good
  cop–bad cop

- The negotiator having his or her own agenda

- Wanting you to start your work before you
  have a contract or even a deal memo

You may have your own additions. Feel free to add to the list or e-mail me with your own personal horror story. Oh, the stories I have heard over the years.

The first thing to remember is that it's not your fault. Many people's immediate reaction to a blowup is, "What did I do wrong?" The answer is probably "nothing" unless you want to count walking into the cage with this untamed tiger without a whip or a chair. Check around. You are not the first person to be exposed to this behavior. You will not be the last.

The second thing to remember is that you can't change this person. Don't even try. These people are who they are. Your job is to conclude this negotiation with a deal or a Walk Away, not to remake this dysfunctional person. Focus on the narrow task of managing the situation, not the person.

The third thing to remember is that you already have wasted too much time thinking about how to wipe out this person (in a bloodless way that leaves no fingerprints, of course). Let it go. Do whatever you have to do to shake off the natural desire to wring the neck of the offender. Maybe a quiet walk in a beautiful garden will do the trick. Maybe you go shopping. Maybe you play computer games. Take whatever kind of break you need to accept the fact that you can't change the other person. Then plan a course of action that is the best way to conclude the negotiation. Don't obsess on doing the other person in, getting even, or spreading the word. The other person will do that on his or her own, given enough time. Just take care of the business at hand and leave it up to the universe to deal with this person.

Exactly how does Wish, Want, Walk help when you find yourself at the negotiating table with a jerk? There are actually two ways in which the Wish-Want-Walk method will help you. First, by having done the work on your Want, you know about (and are forewarned about) your opposite number. Second, by having the plan in your head, you know where the negotiation will end up no matter how outlandish the other person acts.

You Are Forewarned
and Ready

When you set up your Want, you are determining where the negotiation most likely will end up based on a lot of external factors. One of the factors you research is the person with whom you will be negotiating. You are supposed to find out as much as you can about the person who will be across the table. One of the things you are looking for is the reputation of that person in the community. Your research should uncover your counterpart's negotiating style.

A few years ago I was on the same side of an issue as an attorney friend of mine named Paul. He asked me to join him for a meeting with the opposing attorney, about whom I knew nothing at all, although I knew Paul didn't like the way things were going in the negotiation. We were to discuss the upcoming deal. I hadn't done much research because I was there as an observer rather than having to carry the weight of the negotiation. We were in the elevator when my friend said, "I'm so glad you're here. Maybe he won't start yelling." My reaction must have been written all over my face. "Yeah, he's one of those."

The exchange between the two lawyers quickly got testy. Then my friend raised his hand, cocked his thumb, and pointed his finger like the hand puppet of a pistol that every five-year-old knows. He pointed at the other lawyer and said, "You're about to go off, aren't you?" The other lawyer blustered. My friend persisted: "I'm serious. Your face is getting red just like it did in our last meeting."

I was ready to duck under the table. The other lawyer became more flustered, apologized for yelling, and then loudly explained how upset he became every time a certain point was brought up. I didn't necessarily buy his story or his apology, but I was impressed at how being forewarned about the unpleasant style of the opposite party provides a shield of protection against the upset that bad behavior usually causes. Paul was ready for it. He saw it coming, so it didn't throw him off balance.

When you have done your research on the other party, it's not about you anymore. It is about a serious flaw in the other party.

If you know ahead of time that someone is a screamer and that person starts screaming, it is not pleasant, but it is much less unsettling than it otherwise would be. If you know ahead of time that the other person is a bully, you may hate going into the room with him or her, but it doesn't throw you off in the same way that it would if it were a big

Accept the person on the other side of the table as they are; treat the person on the other side of the table as though they were the person you want them to be.

This is very hard to do. The world would be a better place if we could all learn to do it all the time. This is a wish for all of us. In the meantime, all we can do in a negotiation is our best. You will spare yourself great agony if you accept the other person on his or her own terms. Treat those people with the respect they would deserve if they behaved the way you would like them to behave.

surprise. In fact, it is clear to me that the surprise of the situation is one of the things that make the situation difficult. You are as surprised as the deer that is frozen in the headlights of a car, and interestingly, in such a situation your behavior mimics that of the deer. You stop cold in your tracks with your eyes wide open. When you recover your wits, you just want to run.

For instance, I hate being lied to and probably always will. It makes me really angry, except in one situation. If I know ahead of time that I am dealing with a liar, that I can't believe a word that person tells me, it doesn't upset me when he or she operates true to form. I go into the negotiation thinking, "I hate to negotiate with this guy because I know I can't trust him. I don't believe a thing he says. I have to check everything out somewhere else." When the baloney starts flowing, I say to myself, "There he goes again." It doesn't bother me. The reason it doesn't bother me under these circumstances is that I know it is going to happen almost every time I talk to this person. There is no surprise. I am not blindsided. When it doesn't happen, I am pleasantly surprised. Knowing about the person across the table goes a long way toward defusing the situation because it takes away the surprise. You gather information about the personality and style of your opposite number as you prepare your Want. You find out all you can about the other party.

When you do your homework on the opposition, you understand that you are not the only person who thinks this person is a jerk. You are not alone. This is not much solace when you are in the room, trapped in a tirade you don't deserve, being hammered by a lesser human being, embarrassed, mortified, belittled, and befuddled. At least you know that you are not the first person to experience this behavior from this particular person. You are not the last person who will experience this behavior from this particular person. And you are not the only person who finds it extremely objectionable.

Also, with adequate preparation, you understand that it doesn't help to label this person a jerk. These people are who they are. You aren't going to change them. Thank your lucky stars that you are not that person. You do not have to live in that person's skin. You are a good person. You don't treat people like that, and aren't you glad? Clear your head of all that chatter that goes like this: "I am going to get even. I'm going to learn how to be just that obnoxious. I'll show him." He already has been shown up. He already has to live with himself. You don't have to do anything except be the best negotiator you can be.

Hang On to Your Wish, Want, Walk

When you have your Wish, Want, Walk firmly in your head before you start negotiating, you know that the deal will have to fall within those parameters or you will not agree. No matter how the person on the other side of the table may scream or bully or put you down, it is not going to change your Wish, Want, Walk. You know that you are not going back to the office with a deal that is outside the Wish-Want-Walk plan that everybody agreed to before the negotiation started. When you have made your plan beforehand, you may have to waste some time enduring bad behavior, but you won't make a bad deal. If you stick to your Wish, Want, Walk, that can't happen.

You might have thought that you really wanted this deal, but now you have an independent reason not to do the deal with this individual. He or she behaves badly. That creates a toxic atmosphere. You don't want that person in your life. You know now that for the deal to be attractive to you, you will have to close it at the top of your Want or even closer to your Wish, because of the nature of the person across the table. In terms of Figure 2-1 earlier in the book, this person is a real onion. Closing the deal will not turn him or her into a desirable business associate. Now is the time to consider whether or not this may just be the time to Walk.

Your Personal Action Plan

Wish, Want, Walk will not keep your blood pressure down and will not make these nightmare situations be the way you want to spend your afternoons. Here is exactly what you should do in these situations:

- Ask questions.

- Listen.

- Take a break.

These are the three silver bullets you can use in response to unacceptable behavior. They work their magic in a nonthreatening manner. You will see why as you read on.

In the face of unacceptable behavior, the first thing to do is ask questions and listen carefully to the answers. In most instances, you will be well served to do some probing. Find out whatever you can about the statement that surprised you. Showing some genuine interest in the statement can evoke a further explanation. The person already is talking. Get him or her to talk some more. It is a powerful tool. Later, you can review the responses that have been provided. Questions are like trowels in the garden. They help you dig up information, examine the soil, and find out what will make the garden grow.

Asking questions produces much more solid results than trying to make an instantly brilliant definitive statement that leaves the other person without a response, flat-footed, befuddled, and running from the room screaming for help. Only in the movies do those ready responses flow so freely from the lips. Of course, a highly paid script writer had months to come up with the lines that the actor says so spontaneously on screen. You don't have that kind of time. Forget the clever quip. It's not going to happen.

Questions get you past the awkward moment when the other party has stepped over the line. They form a break in the dialogue. The answers should give you some information that will help you build a consensus in spite of the other party's bad behavior.

When you have asked any questions that come to mind at these awkward moments and listened to the response all the way through, take a break. Don't try to be brilliant. Don't come back until you are ready. I call this pushing the pause button.

In a negotiation, the pause button works exactly like the pause button on a DVD player. It freezes everything in place so that we can step away from the negotiation. We can see the picture clearly from every angle. We can leave the room. We can take a break that is as long or short as we need. We can get ready to resume negotiating.

It is our internal pause button that helps us maintain our emotional distance. It is the pause button that prevents us from falling in love with the process so that we lose sight of our Wish, Want, Walk.

Everybody has a pause button. Some people just forget to use it or don't even think about using it in a negotiation. Once you realize what a lifesaver it can be in a negotiation, you will never leave home without it.

In every negotiating seminar, we go around the room and talk about the best way to create a break. People use a wide range of techniques to give themselves room to breath. Some people tell a joke, some "need to go to the bathroom," and some "need to make a phone call." The list is endless.

What is your favorite pause button? Take a moment to think about your own pause buttons. At seminars, participants list a variety of techniques to break things up from telling jokes to asking for a bathroom break—now who could refuse that?

I like to take a break without labeling it in any way. That way, there is no mistake that the reason for the break is the conduct of the other party, not some artificial reason. Whatever works for you to interrupt the flow is what you should do. Do not try to deal with the problem before you take a break. You will not come up quickly with that devastating statement that turns your opponent into a withering mass of Jell-o. Don't even try.

This is also an opportunity to use a tool I've occasionally found effective. It's difficult for some people, but you might want to try it next time you are across the table from a person who is misbehaving. Sometimes, when someone lies, bullies, curses, or screams, I call him or her on it. I tell that person coolly that this behavior is unacceptable and that if it continues, our negotiations will be suspended. Calling a person on bad behavior usually stops it— not always but often enough to make this technique useful. Remember, that person wouldn't be negotiating with you if you didn't have something he or she

Don't just do something, sit there!

When things heat up in
a negotiation, your natural instinct
may be to fight fire with fire.
Usually the best course of action
is not to take any action
or make any response
until you have had time
to ask questions,
listen to the answers
and then take a break
in order to take stock
of the situation.

wanted. These people can rein in their unacceptable behavior if they are convinced that it is in their best interest to do so. If you try this technique, you *must* take a break if the behavior continues. You cannot make idle threats during a negotiation without threatening the entire negotiation and any deal that grows out on it.

Wish, Want, Walk will not insulate you from unpleasant experiences in the negotiating room, but it will help you deal with those situations. It helps you by giving you a framework you can rely on. You simply won't be pushed past your Walk regardless of the trick or tactic or tirade. If you find yourself in such a position, don't try to be a hero. Ask some questions. Listen to the answers. Then take a break. You are not going to change the person on the other side. Your job is to close the deal as soon as possible. Maybe you can send someone else to negotiate with this person next time, but if you do, be sure to warn your replacement.

If you haven't been in one of these tight spots during a negotiation, maybe you are just blessed. But then, why would you be reading this chapter? Or maybe you are a screamer yourself, and you don't mind or notice when someone else screams. If that is the case, your problem is beyond the scope of this book, but I hope—for your sake—that you are working on the problem.

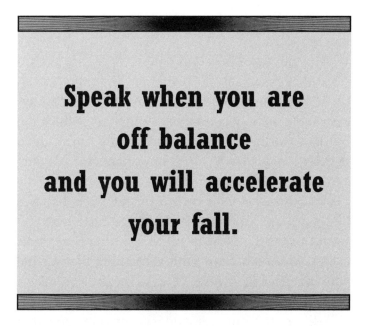

Speak when you are
off balance
and you will accelerate
your fall.

When the Jerk
Is on Your Team

Let's face it. Not all the jerks in the world have been hired by other companies. Sometimes the jerk is sitting next to you, fouling up the deal as surely as if he or she were sitting across the table from you— maybe worse.

You already know who these folks are within your own organization. If it is at all possible, keep them out of negotiating sessions. This is not always easy and generally takes a bit of internal politicking, but it is worth it. Such a person easily can throw a negotiation off track. More important, his conduct can taint your reputation.

When one of your own team members behaves badly, use the same triple-threat response that you would use if the blowup came from the other side, except you might start with something like waving your hands and saying, "Break, break, let's take a break." Keep it light, even humorous, if you can. This will diffuse the situation and let everyone know that this behavior is not the way the rest of the negotiation is going to go.

Before you take a break, however, be sure to implement the triple-threat action plan. Since you can't assume that other negotiators have read this book, you should ask them if they have any questions. Listen to their questions. Make sure that they are answered completely. If they don't ask any questions, feel free to ask (and answer) the questions you think they might want to ask. For instance, you might say something like this: "You may be wondering why Charlie just got so upset. The truth is that this is a touchy topic in our company. So and so was just fired for bringing it up. I'm afraid it's a hot-button issue right now." And then take a break.

What you do about your own jerk (I guess I just gave him the name Charlie) during a break depends a lot on the pecking order in your corporation. If the person is equal to you, have a collegial talk with him about how to behave in a negotiating session. If the person is junior to you, you probably have a greater ability to control the situation. If the person is senior to you, you have a delicate situation, but privately ask questions and listen carefully to the answers.

Just so that you know, it is not uncommon to have the boss be the one who loses composure in a negotiation. Some bosses have less patience and are less informed about the details of the deal. They almost always feel a sense of entitlement to jump into a discussion when it isn't moving fast enough in exactly the direction they think it should go.

In all circumstances, try to reach an agreement during the break about how the rest of the session will go. Try to take charge of the proceedings, with people on your team not speaking unless you call on them. You also might try to schedule a quick adjournment of the session so that you can reschedule the next session, preferably without the explosive element in attendance.

All the situations discussed in this chapter require top leadership and management skills on your part. I wish there were a magic wand I could give you to wave over an unpleasant situation to turn it into an afternoon tea party. There is no such magic wand. You will have to see these situations for the opportunities they are. Each occurrence is a learning opportunity for you. These situations also give you a chance to demonstrate your ability to build consensus, defuse tense situations, and find solutions to problems instead of being distracted by the commotion going on around you. I wouldn't wish such a situation on you or anybody else, but if it occurs, grab the opportunity to shine by being the calming force in the room. Be the person who draws on intelligence and experience to steer through these choppy waters. You will be rewarded—profusely.

Chapter 10

HOW WISH, WANT, WALK HELPS YOU CLOSE THE DEAL

IT IS NO WONDER THAT many people are upset and unsure when it is time to close. Without having their Wish, Want, Walk firmly in hand, they are not sure if they should close the deal. Immediately, their minds race, looking for some magic phrase or groping for some technique to reduce the feeling of unease about closing. The problem does not lie in lacking some skill to close the deal; it lies in being unsure about whether to close the deal at all. That creates a lot of anxiety—high anxiety.

The Wish-Want-Walk method makes it easy to know when you are ready to close. There is no trick to closing. Create a Wish, Want, Walk on all the key points. Be sure you have buy-in from all the people who rightly or wrongly are looking over your shoulder (your boss, your spouse, that snoopy person in the next cubicle). If you are somewhere between your Wish and your Want on a key point, you are ready to close that point and don't have to worry about criticism. If you are between your Want and your Walk on a key point but have been able to push some other point toward your Wish, you know there is balance in the deal and you are ready to close. If you are challenged by someone after the fact, just whip out the old Wish-Want-Walk chart and say, "See how well I did!" Don't let anybody beat you up for a job well done.

The feedback on this point has been immensely satisfying. Once or twice a month, I will be going through my e-mails and there will be a note from someone who took one of my negotiating seminars. These former students write to tell me about the relief they felt using the Wish, Want, Walk method to know when to close a deal. Here are quotes from the last two of those e-mails I received: "It's the first time I felt comfortable closing a deal" and "It seemed so natural, I had to pinch myself. Where was the angst?"

It is easy to understand this reaction in a negotiation with limited issues. If you are buying an automobile or a house, you often find yourself negotiating only about money with whatever variables you can build into the negotiation to expand the pie. More often than not, you can put a dollar value on the things you inject into the negotiation to expand the pie. It is no wonder that Wish, Want, Walk provides so much help in closing those negotiations.

The more interesting feedback came from folks who were involved in more complicated negotiations. Some negotiations have a lot of issues and a number of parties. Those are the cases that typically cause the highest stress levels as the time to close approaches. It turns out that Wish, Want, Walk is most helpful in those situations.

A deal is closed when all the major deal points have been agreed on. Therefore, finding agreement on the major deal points—one by one—and verifying that there is agreement on each one of those deal points are all that is involved in closing a deal no matter how complicated or convoluted the deal may appear to be on the surface. You can always close parts of a deal on your way to closing the entire deal. If there are a number of key points in a negotiation, I make it clear that the overall deal is not closed until we close all the points. I always leave room to go back and revisit a deal point even though we already might have reached tentative agreement on that point. I will revisit something only when another point is not to my satisfaction and I need to improve something else to put the overall deal in balance.

Recall the actual negotiation that we talked about in Chapter 7. I created a chart with six issues for a friend who was negotiating his salary on a new job. He organized them from left to right in their order of priority to him. When I asked him to think about the process a bit more, he came up with two more items that were important to him and added them to the chart. He finished up with eight issues—not bad for a type of negotiation that many people think is all about the money.

This organization of the Wish-Want-Walk chart is important as you negotiate because it helps you keep your priorities straight in your head. It is also helpful when it comes to closing a deal. Let's take another look at that chart, which has been cleaned up to be more generic, as we look at how Wish, Want, Walk helps you close a deal. We will use eight issues. Your next negotiation may have more issues, or it may have fewer. Let's look at those charts to see in a graphic, oversimplified way how all this works out. Let's assume three different situations.

- You are in the Want zone on all issues.

	Issue 1	Issue 2	Issue 3	Issue 4	Issue 5	Issue 6	Issue 7	Issue 8
WISH								
WANT								
WALK								

Figure 10-1

- The best you can do on all the issues is uneven, as indicated below.

	Issue 1	Issue 2	Issue 3	Issue 4	Issue 5	Issue 6	Issue 7	Issue 8
WISH								
WANT								
WALK								

Figure 10-2

- The best you can do on all the issues is uneven, as indicated below.

	Issue 1	Issue 2	Issue 3	Issue 4	Issue 5	Issue 6	Issue 7	Issue 8
WISH								
WANT								
WALK								

Figure 10-3

Obviously, the situations depicted in Figures 10-1 and 10-2 are ready to close. If you organized your priorities correctly, you are unlikely to be enthusiastic about the situation depicted in Figure 10-3. However, that situation is not off the chart, and so it can be closed without violating your Wish, Want, Walk. You will have to push your pause button and decide what needs to change to make this arrangement of results on the various issues attractive to you. That is a deeply personal decision for you and your team. Because it clearly involves trade-offs, you will want to have everyone in on this final decision.

To the extent that the issues can be monetized, you should homogenize them. In other words, money is money, and you don't care where it comes from. If the pay is a bit lower than you want but there are other things being offered that are worth money, such as a car or expenses, consider them all together to figure out if you are in your Want or nearer your Wish or your Walk. The things that cannot be monetized—the intangibles—are more difficult because they are so personal. No one can tell you how you should feel about intangibles such as the title you will be given or the person to whom you will report. That is totally up to you.

In the film business, the intangibles often control the deal. I was brokering a three-way deal among Roy Disney, La Raza Theater, and Ray Bradbury concerning making a film of his famous story "The Ice Cream Suit." I represented the theater. Everyone was happy with the financial terms I had suggested. Things were looking very good as we ate lunch in the executive dining room at the Disney studios in Burbank. However, things turned sour during dessert. Both of these titans wanted final creative control. Neither would budge—not then, not in the months of cajoling that ensued. That important intangible trumped a financial deal that was totally acceptable to everyone involved.

When the opposing party expresses a willingness to accept your position on an issue in the negotiation or you are willing to accept their offer, all you have to do is say something like, "Do we have agreement on that point?" or "Can we agree on that and move on?" Make it clear that the agreement is not final until the entire deal is settled. That is the law. It is also sound negotiating strategy. It is also common courtesy. You give up nothing by making such a statement, and you put the other person at ease, making it easier for that person to nod in agreement at each partial closing point.

Use the same technique if you are not quite ready to commit to the other party on a particular point but are close, and if everything else falls into place, you would be willing to close on that point. Just say so. I usually say something like, "Let's put a pin in this and come back to it after we see where we are on some of these other things." Again, this is a nonconfrontational way to keep things moving. You are not making a commitment, but you are holding out that possibility. A simple straightforward question or statement closes an agreement whether it is a peace treaty after World War II or the purchase of a used car. Closing requires nothing fancy. Closing is not some mysterious act. You just make a simple statement of what is obvious to you because you have established your Wish, Want, Walk.

Often the skill of closing a deal is magnified out of all proportion. Many people feel anxiety about signing off on a deal right around the time they should be feeling satisfaction in getting the deal done. A part of them knows that the deal is ready to close, but the other part of them is saying, "But, what if I am leaving some money on the table? What if there is a better deal out there somewhere? What will my boss say? What will my wife say? What? What? What?"

Part of the problem is that a lot of seminars are devoted to closing a sale or closing a deal. They all try to turn the simple act of verifying that there is agreement on a certain point into a moment of mythical and magical import. Frankly, most of those seminars never take a moment to look at predetermining when to close the deal. Preparing a solid Wish, Want, Walk is the key to avoiding anxiety at the close. No fancy footwork, no quick quip, no tactless trick can substitute for preparation. If you know what you want out of negotiation, you will know when you have it in hand and it is time to close the deal.

It is a tough situation when a deal won't close and the reason that it won't close is that the person on the other side of the table is fixated on his or her hang-ups rather than the substance of the deal. You have to become a temporary shrink to that person and ease him or her through that resistance, that fear of commitment. Every time you sign a contract, you are making a commitment of some sort. If you are negotiating with someone who is commitment-phobic, you have to listen, nudge, and gently press forward. Eventually, the person (or the person's boss) will close the deal. In the meantime, be patient.

How to Walk Away

If you have to walk away in a negotiation, don't do it when you are angry. Hit your pause button. Give yourself some breathing room. If you still feel you want to end the negotiation, do it in a way that will not damage the relationship. This is especially important in a long-term relationship. Never assume that you never again will see the person on the other side of the table, but sometimes the importance of maintaining a relationship is so obvious that you want to pay extra attention to preserving it, not by caving in but by walking away in a classy manner.

I recommend that you write a "wrap-up" letter in which you summarize the final position of the other side "to be sure that you did not misunderstand something" and the final position of your side "in case you didn't communicate it clearly enough." You then summarize your position "to be sure that there was no misunderstanding." Never blame the other person for the breakdown. In fact, you should thank the negotiators for the efforts they made to reach an agreement. Do this even if you think they were being unreasonable at times.

I recommend a letter instead of a phone call because a phone call can prolong a misunderstanding, create new misunderstandings, or needlessly postpone an inevitable decision. Writing a letter allows you to address your views of the negotiation while giving you the time to edit and correct yourself to be sure it is absolutely accurate and unemotional. A letter reduces the chance that the breakdown in the negotiation will be mischaracterized in the future. It also provides a paper trail in case someone else steps in to save the deal. Most important, it allows the other side to say, "Oh, no, you got it all wrong. That's not what I said," or the milder version, "Apparently, I wasn't very clear."

If you receive a conciliatory call from the other side after you walk away, do not argue over whether you "got it right" or "heard it right." Often this sort of call will include a certain amount of put-down. Don't take the bait. Let it go. Such a call is an opportunity to get the negotiation back on track, and that is a good thing.

If you don't receive the call, it's over. It was not meant to be. You have given it your best shot, and there was no deal to be made that you could live with. You walked away with a clear understanding that this was a deal that could not be made with this person at this time.

Congratulations.

Closing is not something you can do by yourself. It takes both sides. You can set up your Wish, your Want, and your Walk all by yourself. You can listen like a sphinx. You can—all by yourself—know when you are ready to close a deal or at least when you are ready to agree on some issue within the deal so that you can move the discussion to another issue in the negotiation. You can present your case passionately and persuasively without much help from the other side.

But you can't close a deal without the other side. It takes two to tango. It takes two to close a deal. This can be quite jangling to some people, so keep asking the other party if you have agreement—point after point after point. As soon as you are satisfied on each succeeding point, move on. When you agree on all points, move on. When you agree on all points, you are finished. That's how you close a deal.

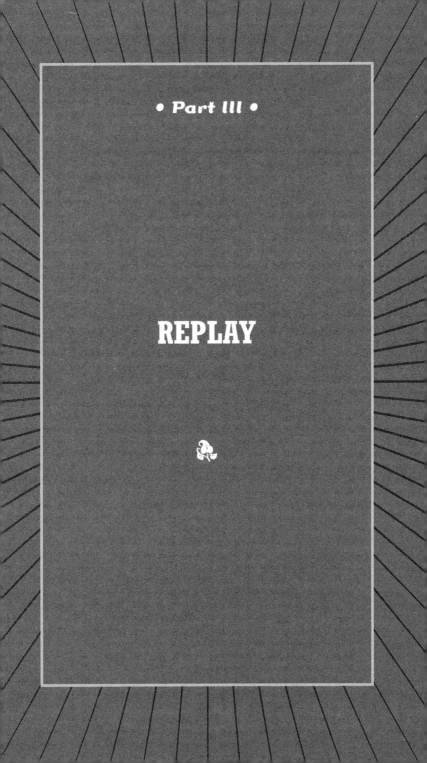

• Part III •

REPLAY

Chapter 11

WISH, WANT, WALK
AS A PREDICTOR

ONCE YOU HAVE SET YOUR Wish, Want, Walk, you and your support team know the range within which the negotiation will end up. You have written down your plan. You will start the negotiation knowing that your first offer will be at or just above your Wish and that you will not agree to anything lower than your Walk-Away point. That leaves a lot of room to close the negotiation. The more you know about the other person's Wish, Want, Walk, the more you can narrow the range within which a negotiation will end up. In fact, in my negotiating seminars, we are able to make an accurate prediction of the results of the mock negotiations we hold.

A mock negotiation is included in all my seminars. One of the most common negotiations involves buying a vase at a flea market. It is a simple 10-minute negotiation after 12 minutes of preparation. Each side is given a short fact sheet. The seminar participants can introduce other terms during the negotiation to keep or obtain a price that is within their Wish, Want, Walk.

Of course, the starting point is to have each of the participants figure out his or her Wish, Want, Walk. I found that the negotiations went better when the participants wrote them out.

A few years ago, I started collecting the Wish, Want, Walk from all the participants after they finished their preparation and before they started the negotiations. My purpose was to save time during the debriefing discussion after the participants had finished the mock negotiation, so I would write the Wish, Want, Walk for each side on flipcharts. It would make reporting back to the class go faster. As I wrote down the various Wish, Want, Walk positions, I tended to mutter to myself that this team wouldn't make a deal because the Wish, Want, Walks of the two negotiators didn't overlap or that team would be finished early because there was a lot of overlap in the Wish, Want, Walks so it would be easy for them to make a deal.

Sure enough, as the participants started drifting back into the seminar room, the first to arrive were the ones I had identified from their Wish-Want-Walk positions as those who would finish early. Most of the ones who did not make a deal had been identified by me from their Wish-Want-Walk positions as not making a deal because there was no overlap between the two sides.

I bet you can do the same thing. Figure 11-1 shows the Wish-Want-Walk positions for even-numbered negotiating teams that participated in a two-day intensive seminar in Portland, Oregon. There were fifteen teams in all. These are the actual results; they have not been tampered with or changed in any way. Read the Wish-Want-Walk positions of the sides as they wrote them down before they started to negotiate with the other side. Fill in your predictions for the various teams. If you think the participants will not reach agreement, check the left column. Otherwise, write down the range within which you think they will agree.

This exercise will take only a minute or two, but it is a real eye-opener. In fact, if you don't have a minute or two right now, try it a little later. It is really worth your time. In every seminar—large or small—the Wish, Want, Walk predicts how the negotiations will turn out with uncanny reliability. Take a moment and fill in the blank spaces in the Figure 11-1. Then we will see how your prediction compared with the real outcomes.

Figure 11-2 shows my predictions before the teams came back into the room. The range of possible agreement is the overlap between the Wish, Want, Walk of the buyer and the Wish, Want, Walk of the seller. Fill in your predictions from Figure 11-1. If your predictions do not match up in most cases with my predictions, take a moment to see why we differed. We should match up pretty closely. It doesn't have to be an exact match. My predictions might be a little broader than yours because I took the widest possible range of agreement according to what the parties said were their Wish, Want, Walk. If your range of most likely outcomes is smaller (or just one number), don't

Team No.		Pre-Negotiation Position		Your Prediction	
		Buyer's Wish, Want, Walk	Seller's Wish, Want, Walk	Participants Won't Agree	Participants Will Agree within This Range
2	Wish	$5	$90		
	Want	$25	$40		
	Walk	$45	$20		
4	Wish	$20	$100		
	Want	$40	$75		
	Walk	$60	$50		
6	Wish	$25	$120		
	Want	$50	$80		
	Walk	$75	$60		
8	Wish	$25	$100		
	Want	$55	$55		
	Walk	$100	$25		
10	Wish	$30	$95		
	Want	$40	$80		
	Walk	$50	$60		
12	Wish	$10	$100		
	Want	$20	$70		
	Walk	$40	$50		
14	Wish	$20	$100		
	Want	$40	$60		
	Walk	$55	$55		

Figure 11-1

Team No.	My Prediction Range of Agreement	Your Prediction Range of Agreement
2	$25–$50	
4	$50–$60	
6	$60–$75	
8	$25–$100	
10	No Agreement	
12	No Agreement	
14	Possible at $55	

Figure 11-2

change it now. You can see how you do against the actual results that are shown in Figure 11-3.

But first compare your predictions with my predictions to be sure that you have the basic concept.

Figure 11-3 shows the actual results. This is the exciting part. The Wish-Want-Walk information acted as a solid predictor of results.

Team No.	My Prediction Range of Agreement	Your Prediction	Actual Outcome
2	$25–$50		$40
4	$50–$60		No Deal
6	$60–$75		$65
8	$25–$100		$50
10	No Agreement		No Deal
12	No Agreement		$60
14	Possible at $55		$55

Figure 11-3

Lessons Learned

Compare what you predicted the results would be with what the results turned out to be.

"Wait, wait," you might say. "Two of them did not match the predictions. What is the story there? Why is that?" Believe me, the class and I asked the same questions. Here are the answers that the team members gave to the entire group in our debriefing session.

Team 4

I predicted that a deal would be made, but it was not. Both sides said that they felt rushed and thought they spent too much of their time on preliminary niceties and getting to know each other. They hadn't budgeted their time closely enough. They thought they would have reached an agreement if they had had more time. In this mock negotiation they knew exactly how much time they had, and thousands of people before them had concluded the negotiation in the exact same amount of allotted time. They should have paced themselves better.

You have to think about the various time constraints as you prepare for a negotiation. That makes a huge difference in resolving issues in an efficient manner. If you fail to keep the time constraints in mind, you find the other side becoming unnecessarily stressed, distracted, or worse. Don't let this happen to you. Time can be your friend or your enemy. Respect the role it plays in every negotiation.

Team 12

I had predicted no deal. Perhaps you did also. The fact that they made a deal surprised me. The buyer changed his Walk number under pressure. He was chagrined. He forgot to write the number down on the piece of paper he was using in the negotiation. Without the numbers being written down, the buyer subconsciously adjusted his Wish, Want, Walk after the seller made a surprisingly high opening demand. The buyer questioned his Wish, Want, Walk and changed it in a flash without really thinking about it. That's a classic "anchor and adjust" situation. The seller anchored the negotiation with a high price, and the buyer instantly adjusted his attitude accordingly. The buyer felt that he would not have agreed to $60 if he had written down his Wish, Want, Walk. He vowed to be more careful in the future. A valuable lesson was learned.

This negotiation has been done with groups as small as 9 and as large as 200. The results are predicted by the original Wish-Want-Walk numbers in almost all the cases. When the results don't match the predictions, there is always a real-world lesson to be learned.

When the negotiations result in an agreement, the participants begin to discern a pattern in the results. It turns out that the sellers who set their Wish price for the vase higher than the group average almost always achieve a higher final sales price. Buyers who set their Wish at the lower price average ended up closing the negotiation on a lower than average number. We talk about this before they go into their mock negotiations, but seeing it actually happen time after time is a real eye-opener.

The group of participants also gets to see first-hand the dynamics when the seller's Wish for a price and the Buyer's Wish for a price are far apart. In these cases, it frequently takes a long time to reach a final settlement. When the buyer and the seller have pre-set their Wishes so that they are close together, the settlement typically comes quickly. In these cases, the final settlement tends to fall almost squarely in the middle of the two numbers.

The importance of spending time in the preparation stage of the negotiation is abundantly clear when the results of the mock negotiation are laid out on a chart. Your Wish, Want, Walk has a greater effect on the outcome of the negotiation than your personality or any trick or technique you might hear about. If you take nothing else away from this book, know that a solid Wish, Want, Walk is the best foundation for a successful negotiation.

Chapter 12

MEASURING SUCCESS WITH WISH, WANT, WALK

ONE OF THE BEST THINGS about writing down your Wish, Want, Walk before starting a negotiation is that it provides a way for you to judge objectively how you did in the negotiation. To know whether you did well in a negotiation, do not look at how others did. Judge the result against your own Wish, Want, Walk.

The Dalai Lama wrote a wonderful book titled *The Pursuit of Happiness*. The thesis of the book is that happiness should be the purpose of everyone's life and that everyone has a right, not a duty, to be happy. Our own Declaration of Independence refers to the pursuit of happiness as an inalienable right. You cannot consider yourself a success in life if you have not achieved happiness.

The Dalai Lama also says that we should not look at other people to determine our happiness. One of the greatest impediments to happiness is comparing ourselves to others. He says that if you compare yourself to others, you will always be unhappy. There is always someone who has more of what you want in life than you do. My corollary to the Dalai Lama's teaching is that there is always someone who bought for a little less or sold for a little more.

Let's talk about who the best negotiators were in that mock negotiation we analyzed in Chapter 11 from the point of view of predicting results. Each participant who played the role of the buyer received the same fact sheet as the other buyers, and each participant who played the role of the seller received the same fact sheet as the other sellers. They all had the same amount of time to read their fact sheets and establish a Wish, Want, Walk. Each team had the same amount of time to negotiate.

Let's do some direct comparisons. How would you rank the buyers in each of the following three teams in terms of how they negotiated their deals? Which buyer was the best negotiator? Which buyer was the weakest negotiator?

Team Number	Negotiated Price
2	$40
8	$50
14	$55

Based solely on the actual results, most people would rank the skills of the buyers in the order in which they are listed. Most people pick the buyer in team 2 as the best negotiator because he paid only $40. Who did you pick? Most people pick the buyer in team 14 as the weakest because he paid $55 for the vase. What do you think? You may want to review the Wish-Want-Walk positions of the parties before answering. For your convenience, Figure 12-1 summarizes the information provided in Chapter 11.

Team No.		Pre-Negotiation		My Prediction	Your Prediction	Actual Outcome
		Buyer WWW	Seller WWW			
2	Wish	$5	$90	$25–$50		$40
	Want	$25	$40			
	Walk	$45	$20			
8	Wish	$25	$100	$25–$100		$50
	Want	$55	$55			
	Walk	$100	$25			
14	Wish	$20	$100	Possible at $55		$55
	Want	$40	$60			
	Walk	$55	$55			

Figure 11-1

When you see the facts in chart form, you realize that the toughest negotiation (for both sides) was the one involving team 14. The buyer's Walk was the same as the seller's Walk. That point was exactly $55—not one penny more or one penny less. A price of $55 was the exact point where a deal could be made unless one or the other caved in on the preset

Walk number. It took a great deal of skill on the part of the buyer and the seller for them to find that point and make a deal at all. Both negotiators on that team took away the prize for a job well done. The buyer paid the most of anyone in the class, but he was the only buyer to talk the seller into selling at exactly the seller's Walk-Away point.

Note that buyer 2 (the one with the best-looking result) was near his Walk-Away point, whereas the seller in that negotiation was right where he expected to be and had quite a bit of room if he needed to reduce the price a bit to make the sale. It turned out that the seller was a very tough negotiator and began giving up ground very grudgingly long before he was near his Walk-Away point. In fact, he gave up grudgingly as they were approaching his Want number, whereas the buyer moved quickly to his Want number and attempted to hold ground there but could not. In terms of using his negotiating skills, buyer 2's performance as a negotiator was the weakest of the three buyers even though he paid the least for the vase.

Buyer 8, in contrast, was able to negotiate the seller below his Want, approaching the seller's Walk number while he himself was still on the Wish side of his Want number. His performance was very good. We know that because we know the Wish, Want, Walk of both sides, not because of the outcome of the negotiation in terms of the dollars paid for the vase. Team 8's negotiation also turned out to be the least stressful negotiation for the two participants because they both had the same expectation of where the negotiation should end up. That is, they had the same Want.

In this totally artificial environment, the participants negotiated hard. Some emotions flared. When the dust settled and the results were in, the results were quite different even though all the buyers received the same briefing sheet and all the sellers received the same briefing sheet. When the participants came back into the room after the mock negotiation, they were satisfied with the results they had achieved. Everybody is happy at this point. But as we begin gathering the results from various participants, the groans are audible when someone reports that he or she got a much better price as a seller or paid a lot less as a buyer than the person doing the groaning. I try to orchestrate the order of the reports so that the sales number keeps getting higher.

Just as the class is whooping it up for the seller who got the highest price for the vase, we deliver one of the most important lessons of the session by examining the results in greater detail. What looks like a spectacularly good outcome may not be that good when it is measured against the original Wish-Want-Walk positions that each of the parties set out before the negotiation started. Buyer 8 paid more but negotiated very skillfully. Buyer 2, who paid the least of the three, actually was outnegotiated by the seller. The circumstances of their negotiations were different.

Our classroom analysis then moved on to why seller 2 put such a low value on the vase. His negotiating skills were terrific, but perhaps he needed to work harder in the preparation stage. Seller 2 had the lowest Want and Walk in the group. In light of his skills in the negotiating session, he surely would have sold the vase for more money if his initial numbers had been higher.

One thing that should be crystal clear by now is the importance of where you set your Wish, Want, Walk and how influential that is on the entire negotiating process. Take great care in setting those numbers. They really do affect the outcome. In fact, they influence the outcome as much as or more than anything you say in the room. Wish, Want, Walk also gives you a legitimate way to judge yourself and others when it comes to a negotiation. Don't automatically assume that the buyer who paid the lowest price conducted the best negotiation. And don't look at the results of others to judge your own skills.

If you bought a three-year-old black Thunderbird convertible for $24,000 and your friend bought a three-year-old black Thunderbird convertible for $20,000, that does not make your friend a better negotiator. What if you bought your car from someone who was emotionally attached to it and didn't want to sell it at any price, certainly not for less than $25,000? And what if your friend bought the car from someone who was in financial trouble and would have taken $15,000 because he was about to lose his house? With that added information, it is clear that you did a much better job negotiating even though your friend paid $4,000 less.

Don't judge the skills of a negotiator only by the result without having a lot of information about the situations of each of the negotiators. This simple fact is enormously helpful to younger members of your organization as they gain experience in negotiating. Don't let them beat themselves up if their outcome wasn't as good as someone else's. Focus on the pre-set Wish, Want, Walk. Also consider whatever information you have about the other side. That is how you evaluate negotiating skills objectively.

After you complete your next negotiation, refer to the paper where you wrote down your own Wish, Want, Walk. If someone comes up and says, "Well, I only paid $X for that," it doesn't make that person a better negotiator. Your situation was different. Maybe you had ten minutes to get home for a birthday celebration and needed to get something quickly.

Think about what might have been different— how you might change the way you negotiate the next time you are in a similar situation. Sometimes you have the special privilege of a celebratory drink with the other side after a negotiation is completed. When that happens, you sometimes can learn valuable lessons about how to conduct the next negotiation with that person. Your collegial review of the process can be like a graduate course in negotiating with that particular person. Even if you are all alone after a negotiating session, there is a real payoff to reviewing the entire process quietly against the negotiating approach you followed in the negotiation.

As you ponder how you might have altered the outcome, do not be greedy. If the deal you made was fair, you have contributed to your long-term working relationship with the other person. In trying to figure out how you could have done better, the answer almost always is found in the questions, "What could I have known before starting this negotiation that I did not know?" and "What questions could I have asked?"

The most important factor that could have created a better result in any specific negotiation usually does not take place in the negotiating room. It is rare that you could have changed the final outcome of the negotiation by saying something better, more cleverly, or with a bit of a twist. What you set down as your Wish, Want, Walk is what will influence the outcome. Anything that you find out from the other person during the negotiating session improves your ability to negotiate an even better deal for your side and sometimes for the other side also. The questions you ask and the information you gain will alter the course of the negotiation. However, the course of the negotiation is set by your Wish, Want, Walk. Your Wish and your Walk define the outer limits of the negotiation before the negotiation begins.

Chapter 13

WRAPPING IT UP

HERE ARE THE HIGHLIGHTS OF THIS BOOK:

The book is about a simple method that guides you toward agreements that work. This method asks you to create your **Wish**, your **Want**, and your **Walk** *before* you start negotiating. It lets you negotiate without fear or apprehension.

You can rely on this simple method in a single-issue negotiation and in the most complex, complicated, convoluted cockamamie concoction of issues you ever saw. It doesn't matter what subject you are negotiating about next. Whatever it is you are negotiating, I define negotiation broadly to include any time that:

• You ask someone to agree to something.

• You ask someone to do something.

• You ask someone to get out of your way so that you can do it yourself

Take the time to create your Wish, Want, Walk.

Creating your Wish and setting your Walk are intensely personal propositions. Some information can be helpful to keep these items realistic, but ultimately these two points defy a popularity poll. You need to satisfy yourself and be comfortable with these two items that bracket the negotiation no matter what anybody else says. You are your own person. Do not get pulled off target by the ideas somebody else might have for you about the goals you should set for yourself or the point at which you should walk away from a deal.

Understanding Want, however, requires a lot of input from a lot of people and resources. You need to know the marketplace or you will have no solid basis for predicting where the deal will close. Gather information steadily and over as long a period as possible. It is often said, "The one with the most information wins."

Knowing your Wish, setting your Walk Away on each issue in the negotiation, and understanding Want (the most likely marketplace results) builds confidence. The trick, if there is one, is to take sufficient time in creating your Wish, Want, Walk. This is not a casual exercise. It is worth your time to create a Wish, Want, Walk because it will guide you through the entire negotiation. If you invest adequate time in this essential step, you will reap big dividends.

Once you have built a strong foundation for the negotiation by setting your Wish, Want, Walk, you are ready to go into the negotiating room. Wish, Want, Walk will guide you every step of the way. Wish, Want, Walk determines your opening offer. It gives you comfort when you know the negotiation is in your Want zone. It creates an automatic line of resistance when the negotiation gets too close to your Walk-Away point. It guides you as you seek and yield concessions. It affects the pace of the negotiation at every stage. It lets you know when you can close a deal with pride, without worrying about whether you can squeeze another nickel out of the deal. Most important, it lets you know when you have to walk away from a deal and leave it for someone else who has a different Wish, Want, Walk.

Having a plan that everyone agrees on goes a long way toward giving you confidence. It allows you to sit quietly and do the most important thing negotiators can do when they are in the negotiating room: listen.

Listen to the person on the other side of the table. Listen with your ears and your eyes and with every pore of your body. Soak up the viewpoint of the other person. The only way you can find a match is to understand what the other party is seeking. When you are listening, you are building a special rapport with the other person. You aren't giving ground and aren't conceding a thing. You are learning what the other side wants. Because you have your Wish, Want, Walk firmly in hand, you do not have to worry about making a bad deal. You and your team already have decided what you can and can't do in this negotiation. By listening to the other party, you will find out what that person can and can't do. Then you fit the pieces together to make the best deal possible from your perspective.

Perhaps as important as anything in this book, *trust your instincts.*

When you have established a well-thought-out Wish, Want, Walk, you will find that your instincts kick in at the opportune time. Instincts are not a substitute for good solid preparation, but they send strong signals to you once you are in the negotiating room with your Wish, Want, Walk firmly in hand. They are your own personal guideposts, different from the instincts of everyone else on the planet. You have built them over a lifetime of experience. Trust them. Use them.

Scientists are studying the source of instinct, which lies deep within the brain. You and I just have to learn to trust it. Your instinct will guide you through the choppiest waters.

All of this may sound like hard work to a lot of people. Where are the tricks? Where are the gimmicks? You spent good money on this book (or are you still standing in the bookstore reading it for free?). You want a gimmick. Well, go to the gimmick store. If you want to negotiate a solid deal every time, spend time creating a solid Wish, Want, Walk.

And when it is all over, the two most important things are

your integrity

and your reputation.

"It takes 60 years to build
a reputation;
It can be destroyed in
60 seconds."

–Warren Buffett

Having a Wish, Want, Walk plan will provide you with the advantage of feeling comfortable throughout the negotiation process. There will also be frustrations.

There will be lots of frustration when you sit down with someone who is not a good listener and have to repeat yourself three or four times when you try to make a point.

There will be lots of frustration when the other side doesn't know much about the subject of the negotiation and you have to spend time to educate them.

There will be lots of frustrations when the other party doesn't have a clear Wish, Want, Walk and you feel that you are doing all the work for them.

Your greatest success will come when you share everything in this book with each person with whom you negotiate. You have received a gift. The more you share it with your coworkers and those on the opposite side of the table, the more you will grow in your own skills. Never treat knowledge as a secret. Share everything you have learned. The more the other party follows the approach of this book, the faster your negotiation will come to a successful close. Then you can take time to smell the roses.

The beauty of

Wish, Want, Walk

is that it works best

when both sides use it.

SHARE IT!!!

ACKNOWLEDGMENTS

Betsy Redfern has been a mentor and supporter of enormous importance in my life. I had occasionally taught negotiating skills at UCLA, but had determinedly avoided the commercial world, because I enjoyed my own law practice so much. Betsy single-handedly convinced me to start teaching an intensive negotiating course at MWH, Global, one of the world's leading engineering companies. This course led to an active practice of consulting and seminars.

The participants in these various seminars always contribute a lot, whether at MWH headquarters in Denver, Colorado, or in Asia or Europe, or in the academic climes of UCLA, USC, or the Binger Institute in Amsterdam or at dot.coms in the Northwest. In fact, I never go away from a seminar without having learned something. There are always new insights, new ways to phrase things, new questions to be answered.

Gus Avila was the real anchor for getting this book delivered on time to McGraw-Hill. His uncanny ability to read my hen-scratching, his fast turnaround on every draft, and his keen eye for detail were the factors that made it happen. He saw so many drafts over the course of the two years that this book was in development that he probably recited it in his sleep. Needless to say, Herb Schaffner, publisher of McGraw-Hill Business Books (and editor of this book) and his entire crew were happy that Gus was in the picture. And, of course, the art department did a terrific job on the cover. The publicity and marketing departments are responsible for the success of the book in the marketplace. Thanks to Eileen Lamadore, Tara Cibelli, and Lydia Rinaldi. They are supported by Ferrazzi Greenlight: Ken Gillett, Peter Winick, Nam Bui, Love Streams, and Keith Ferrazzi.

Every author feels special appreciation to those who read drafts of a book: Betsy Redfern, Jim Kuiken, Catherine Goddard, and Vince Ravine. Many chores at my law office that would normally be my responsibility were artfully overseen by Jeremy Moehlmann, Vince Ravine, Katheleen Ebora, Ryann Gooden, Zach Zyskowski, and Mart Wallerstein.

My three girls—Michelle, Amy and Wendy—are grown and out of the house now, but their lasting lessons will always be with me. They are each with outstanding men—Ray Rapko, Eddie Graham and John Friess. Then there is our grandson, Soul, whose clarity and integrity gives new meaning to the value-oriented negotiating that drives this book. He knows what he wants. He is never afraid to state his Wish. He makes his position very clear before he Walks. And he is not afraid to Walk out of a negotiation if it doesn't go well. He will be passing this wisdom on to his new cousin Caden.

And of course Tim Kittleson, who not only read the manuscript at its early and late stages, but did much, much more—all along the way—to make this book happen on time and on target.

ABOUT THE AUTHOR

Michael C. Donaldson is an ex-Marine and competitive gymnast whose entertainment law practice has led him to write about and teach negotiating skills around the world. He has been cochair of the Entertainment Section of the Beverly Hills Bar Association and is listed on Who's Who in American Law. He has negotiated for and against some of the biggest names in Hollywood. He also serves as General Counsel to several nonprofit theater and film organizations, including Film Independent. His negotiating seminars and speeches have been hear across America and in Europe and Asia. He can also be reached at:

Michael C. Donaldson
2118 Wilshire Blvd., Ste. 500
Santa Monica, CA 90406-5784
Or: michael@michaeldonaldson.com

FREE NEGOTIATING STUFF!

Fill out this coupon to receive the following:

- **FREE: Ten Ways to Become a Master Negotiator.** Use this downloadable model as a reference tool to reinforce the key takeaways from the book

- **FREE: Ten-Step Preparation Sheet** to prepare you and your team for any negotiation

- **FREE: Ten Common Negotiating Mistakes**

- **20% Discount** on a 1-hour Negotiating DVD by Michael Donaldson.

www.WishWantWalk.com

☐ **YES!** Send me my three **FREE** resources and my **20% discount.**

☐ **YES!** Please keep me informed about Michael Donaldson's **latest** on negotiating.

NAME _____

COMPANY _____

ADDRESS _____

CITY _____ STATE _____ ZIP _____

EMAIL (Required Field)* _____

*Your F R E E resources will be delivered via email confirmation.

Michael C. Donaldson

Resource Fulfillment Center

2118 W. Wilshire Blvd., #500

Santa Monica, CA 90403